GNU Screen - The virtual terminal manager

A catalogue record for this book is available from the Hong Kong Public Libraries.

Published in Hong Kong by Samurai Media Limited.

Email: info@samuraimedia.org

ISBN 978-988-8381-39-5

1 Overview

Screen is a full-screen window manager that multiplexes a physical terminal between several processes, typically interactive shells. Each virtual terminal provides the functions of the DEC VT100 terminal and, in addition, several control functions from the ISO 6429 (ECMA 48, ANSI X3.64) and ISO 2022 standards (e.g. insert/delete line and support for multiple character sets). There is a scrollback history buffer for each virtual terminal and a copy-and-paste mechanism that allows the user to move text regions between windows.

When `screen` is called, it creates a single window with a shell in it (or the specified command) and then gets out of your way so that you can use the program as you normally would. Then, at any time, you can create new (full-screen) windows with other programs in them (including more shells), kill the current window, view a list of the active windows, turn output logging on and off, copy text between windows, view the scrollback history, switch between windows, etc. All windows run their programs completely independent of each other. Programs continue to run when their window is currently not visible and even when the whole screen session is detached from the user's terminal.

When a program terminates, `screen` (per default) kills the window that contained it. If this window was in the foreground, the display switches to the previously displayed window; if none are left, `screen` exits.

Everything you type is sent to the program running in the current window. The only exception to this is the one keystroke that is used to initiate a command to the window manager. By default, each command begins with a control-a (abbreviated `C-a` from now on), and is followed by one other keystroke. The command character (see Section 14.3 [Command Character], page 64) and all the key bindings (see Chapter 14 [Key Binding], page 63) can be fully customized to be anything you like, though they are always two characters in length.

`Screen` does not understand the prefix `C-` to mean control. Please use the caret notation (`^A` instead of `C-a`) as arguments to e.g. the `escape` command or the `-e` option. `Screen` will also print out control characters in caret notation.

The standard way to create a new window is to type `C-a c`. This creates a new window running a shell and switches to that window immediately, regardless of the state of the process running in the current window. Similarly, you can create a new window with a custom command in it by first binding the command to a keystroke (in your '`.screenrc`' file or at the `C-a :` command line) and then using it just like the `C-a c` command. In addition, new windows can be created by running a command like:

```
screen emacs prog.c
```

from a shell prompt within a previously created window. This will not run another copy of `screen`, but will instead supply the command name and its arguments to the window manager (specified in the $STY environment variable) who will use it to create the new window. The above example would start the `emacs` editor (editing '`prog.c`') and switch to its window.

If '`/etc/utmp`' is writable by `screen`, an appropriate record will be written to this file for each window, and removed when the window is closed. This is useful for working with `talk`, `script`, `shutdown`, `rsend`, `sccs` and other similar programs that use the utmp file to determine who you are. As long as **screen** is active on your terminal, the terminal's own record is removed from the utmp file. See Section 10.4 [Login], page 41.

2 Getting Started

Before you begin to use screen you'll need to make sure you have correctly selected your terminal type, just as you would for any other termcap/terminfo program. (You can do this by using tset, qterm, or just set term=mytermtype, for example.)

If you're impatient and want to get started without doing a lot more reading, you should remember this one command: C-a ? (see Chapter 14 [Key Binding], page 63). Typing these two characters will display a list of the available screen commands and their bindings. Each keystroke is discussed in the section on keystrokes (see Section 5.1 [Default Key Bindings], page 11). Another section (see Chapter 4 [Customization], page 9) deals with the contents of your '.screenrc'.

If your terminal is a "true" auto-margin terminal (it doesn't allow the last position on the screen to be updated without scrolling the screen) consider using a version of your terminal's termcap that has automatic margins turned *off*. This will ensure an accurate and optimal update of the screen in all circumstances. Most terminals nowadays have "magic" margins (automatic margins plus usable last column). This is the VT100 style type and perfectly suited for screen. If all you've got is a "true" auto-margin terminal screen will be content to use it, but updating a character put into the last position on the screen may not be possible until the screen scrolls or the character is moved into a safe position in some other way. This delay can be shortened by using a terminal with insert-character capability.

See Section 16.5 [Special Capabilities], page 72, for more information about telling screen what kind of terminal you have.

3 Invoking Screen

Screen has the following command-line options:

'-a'   Include *all* capabilities (with some minor exceptions) in each window's term-cap, even if screen must redraw parts of the display in order to implement a function.

'-A'   Adapt the sizes of all windows to the size of the display. By default, screen may try to restore its old window sizes when attaching to resizable terminals (those with 'WS' in their descriptions, e.g. suncmd or some varieties of xterm).

'-c file'   Use *file* as the user's configuration file instead of the default of '$HOME/.screenrc'.

'-d [pid.sessionname]'
'-D [pid.sessionname]'
            Do not start screen, but instead detach a screen session running elsewhere (see Section 8.1 [Detach], page 31). '-d' has the same effect as typing C-a d from the controlling terminal for the session. '-D' is the equivalent to the power detach key. If no session can be detached, this option is ignored. In combination with the -r/-R option more powerful effects can be achieved:

            -d -r   Reattach a session and if necessary detach it first.

            -d -R   Reattach a session and if necessary detach or even create it first.

            -d -RR   Reattach a session and if necessary detach or create it. Use the first session if more than one session is available.

            -D -r   Reattach a session. If necessary detach and logout remotely first.

            -D -R   Attach here and now. In detail this means: If a session is running, then reattach. If necessary detach and logout remotely first. If it was not running create it and notify the user. This is the author's favorite.

            -D -RR   Attach here and now. Whatever that means, just do it.

            Note: It is a good idea to check the status of your sessions with screen -list before using this option.

'-e xy'   Set the command character to x, and the character generating a literal command character (when typed after the command character) to y. The defaults are C-a and a, which can be specified as '-e^Aa'. When creating a screen session, this option sets the default command character. In a multiuser session all users added will start off with this command character. But when attaching to an already running session, this option only changes the command character of the attaching user. This option is equivalent to the commands defescape or escape respectively. (see Section 14.3 [Command Character], page 64).

'-f'
'-fn'
'-fa'   Set flow-control to on, off, or automatic switching mode, respectively. This option is equivalent to the defflow command (see Chapter 15 [Flow Control], page 67).

'-h *num*'   Set the history scrollback buffer to be *num* lines high. Equivalent to the **defscrollback** command (see Section 12.1 [Copy], page 55).

'-i'   Cause the interrupt key (usually *C-c*) to interrupt the display immediately when flow control is on. This option is equivalent to the **interrupt** argument to the **defflow** command (see Chapter 15 [Flow Control], page 67). Its use is discouraged.

'-l'
'-ln'   Turn login mode on or off (for '/etc/utmp' updating). This option is equivalent to the **deflogin** command (see Section 10.4 [Login], page 41).

'-ls [*match*]'
'-list [*match*]'
             Do not start **screen**, but instead print a list of session identification strings (usually of the form *pid.tty.host*; see Section 8.5 [Session Name], page 34). Sessions marked 'detached' can be resumed with **screen -r**. Those marked 'attached' are running and have a controlling terminal. If the session runs in multiuser mode, it is marked 'multi'. Sessions marked as 'unreachable' either live on a different host or are dead. An unreachable session is considered dead, when its name matches either the name of the local host, or the specified parameter, if any. See the -r flag for a description how to construct matches. Sessions marked as 'dead' should be thoroughly checked and removed. Ask your system administrator if you are not sure. Remove sessions with the '-wipe' option.

'-L'   Tell **screen** to turn on automatic output logging for the windows.

'-m'   Tell **screen** to ignore the $STY environment variable. When this option is used, a new session will always be created, regardless of whether **screen** is being called from within another **screen** session or not. This flag has a special meaning in connection with the '-d' option:

             -d -m   Start **screen** in *detached* mode. This creates a new session but doesn't attach to it. This is useful for system startup scripts.

             -D -m   This also starts **screen** in *detached* mode, but doesn't fork a new process. The command exits if the session terminates.

'-p *name_or_number*'
             Preselect a window. This is useful when you want to reattach to a specific window or you want to send a command via the '-X' option to a specific window. As with screen's select command, '-' selects the blank window. As a special case for reattach, '=' brings up the windowlist on the blank window.

'-q'   Suppress printing of error messages. In combination with '-ls' the exit value is set as follows: 9 indicates a directory without sessions. 10 indicates a directory with running but not attachable sessions. 11 (or more) indicates 1 (or more) usable sessions. In combination with '-r' the exit value is as follows: 10 indicates that there is no session to resume. 12 (or more) indicates that there are 2 (or more) sessions to resume and you should specify which one to choose. In all other cases '-q' has no effect.

'`-r [pid.sessionname]`'

'`-r sessionowner/[pid.sessionname]`'

Resume a detached **screen** session. No other options (except combinations with '-d' or '-D') may be specified, though the session name (see Section 8.5 [Session Name], page 34) may be needed to distinguish between multiple detached **screen** sessions. The second form is used to connect to another user's screen session which runs in multiuser mode. This indicates that screen should look for sessions in another user's directory. This requires setuid-root.

'`-R`'   Resume the first appropriate detached **screen** session. If successful, all other command-line options are ignored. If no detached session exists, start a new session using the specified options, just as if '-R' had not been specified. This option is set by default if screen is run as a login-shell (actually screen uses '-xRR' in that case). For combinations with the '-D'/'-d' option see there.

'`-s program`'

Set the default shell to be *program*. By default, **screen** uses the value of the environment variable $SHELL, or '/bin/sh' if it is not defined. This option is equivalent to the **shell** command (see Section 6.4 [Shell], page 26).

'`-S sessionname`'

Set the name of the new session to *sessionname*. This option can be used to specify a meaningful name for the session in place of the default *tty.host* suffix. This name identifies the session for the **screen -list** and **screen -r** commands. This option is equivalent to the **sessionname** command (see Section 8.5 [Session Name], page 34).

'`-t name`'   Set the title (name) for the default shell or specified program. This option is equivalent to the **shelltitle** command (see Section 6.4 [Shell], page 26).

'`-U`'   Run screen in UTF-8 mode. This option tells screen that your terminal sends and understands UTF-8 encoded characters. It also sets the default encoding for new windows to '`utf8`'.

'`-v`'   Print the version number.

'`-wipe [match]`'

List available screens like **screen -ls**, but remove destroyed sessions instead of marking them as '`dead`'. An unreachable session is considered dead, when its name matches either the name of the local host, or the explicitly given parameter, if any. See the -r flag for a description how to construct matches.

'`-x`'   Attach to a session which is already attached elsewhere (multi-display mode). **Screen** refuses to attach from within itself. But when cascading multiple screens, loops are not detected; take care.

'`-X`'   Send the specified command to a running screen session. You can use the -d or -r option to tell screen to look only for attached or detached screen sessions. Note that this command doesn't work if the session is password protected.

4 Customizing Screen

You can modify the default settings for `screen` to fit your tastes either through a personal '`.screenrc`' file which contains commands to be executed at startup, or on the fly using the `colon` command.

4.1 The '`.screenrc`' file

When `screen` is invoked, it executes initialization commands from the files '`.screenrc`' in the user's home directory and '`/usr/local/etc/screenrc`'. These defaults can be overridden in the following ways: For the global screenrc file `screen` searches for the environment variable `$SYSSCREENRC` (this override feature may be disabled at compile-time). The user specific screenrc file is searched for in `$SCREENRC`, then '`$HOME/.screenrc`'. The command line option '`-c`' specifies which file to use (see Chapter 3 [Invoking Screen], page 5. Commands in these files are used to set options, bind commands to keys, and to automatically establish one or more windows at the beginning of your `screen` session. Commands are listed one per line, with empty lines being ignored. A command's arguments are separated by tabs or spaces, and may be surrounded by single or double quotes. A '#' turns the rest of the line into a comment, except in quotes. Unintelligible lines are warned about and ignored. Commands may contain references to environment variables. The syntax is the shell-like `$VAR` or `${VAR}`. Note that this causes incompatibility with previous `screen` versions, as now the '$'-character has to be protected with '\' if no variable substitution is intended. A string in single-quotes is also protected from variable substitution.

Two configuration files are shipped as examples with your screen distribution: '`etc/screenrc`' and '`etc/etcscreenrc`'. They contain a number of useful examples for various commands.

4.2 Source

source *file* [Command]

    (none)

    Read and execute commands from file *file*. Source commands may be nested to a maximum recursion level of ten. If *file* is not an absolute path and screen is already processing a source command, the parent directory of the running source command file is used to search for the new command file before screen's current directory.

    Note that termcap/terminfo/termcapinfo commands only work at startup and reattach time, so they must be reached via the default screenrc files to have an effect.

4.3 Colon

Customization can also be done online, with this command:

colon [Command]

    (`C-a :`)

    Allows you to enter '`.screenrc`' command lines. Useful for on-the-fly modification of key bindings, specific window creation and changing settings. Note that the **set** keyword no longer exists, as of version 3.3. Change default settings with commands starting with 'def'. You might think of this as the ex command mode of screen, with copy as its vi command mode (see Chapter 12 [Copy and Paste], page 55).

5 Commands

A command in `screen` can either be bound to a key, invoked from a screenrc file, or called from the `colon` prompt (see Chapter 4 [Customization], page 9). As of version 3.3, all commands can be bound to keys, although some may be less useful than others. For a number of real life working examples of the most important commands see the files 'etc/screenrc' and 'etc/etcscreenrc' of your screen distribution.

In this manual, a command definition looks like this:

– Command: command [-n] ARG1 [ARG2] . . .
      (*keybindings*)
      This command does something, but I can't remember what.

An argument in square brackets ('[]') is optional. Many commands take an argument of 'on' or 'off', which is indicated as *state* in the definition.

5.1 Default Key Bindings

As mentioned previously, each keyboard command consists of a *C-a* followed by one other character. For your convenience, all commands that are bound to lower-case letters are also bound to their control character counterparts (with the exception of *C-a a*; see below). Thus, both *C-a c* and *C-a C-c* can be used to create a window.

The following table shows the default key bindings:

C-a '   (select)
                 Prompt for a window identifier and switch. See Chapter 7 [Selecting], page 29.

C-a "   (windowlist -b)
                 Present a list of all windows for selection. See Chapter 7 [Selecting], page 29.

C-a 0...9, -
                 (select 0. . . select 9, select -)
                 Switch to window number 0. . . 9, or the blank window. See Chapter 7 [Selecting], page 29.

C-a TAB   (focus)
                 Switch the input focus to the next region. See Chapter 9 [Regions], page 37.

C-a C-a   (other)
                 Toggle to the window displayed previously. If this window does no longer exist, **other** has the same effect as **next**. See Chapter 7 [Selecting], page 29.

C-a a   (meta)
                 Send the command character (C-a) to window. See **escape** command. See Section 14.3 [Command Character], page 64.

C-a A   (title)
                 Allow the user to enter a title for the current window. See Section 10.1 [Naming Windows], page 39.

C-a b
C-a C-b   (break)
                 Send a break to the tty. See Section 20.2 [Break], page 81.

C-a B   (pow_break)
             Close and reopen the tty-line. See Section 20.2 [Break], page 81.

C-a c
C-a C-c   (screen)
             Create a new window with a shell and switch to that window. See Section 6.2
             [Screen Command], page 25.

C-a C   (clear)
             Clear the screen. See Section 11.5 [Clear], page 50.

C-a d
C-a C-d   (detach)
             Detach **screen** from this terminal. See Section 8.1 [Detach], page 31.

C-a D D   (pow_detach)
             Detach and logout. See Section 8.2 [Power Detach], page 31.

C-a f
C-a C-f   (flow)
             Cycle flow among 'on', 'off' or 'auto'. See Section 15.2 [Flow], page 67.

C-a F   (fit)
             Resize the window to the current region size. See Section 11.10 [Window Size],
             page 52.

C-a C-g   (vbell)
             Toggle visual bell mode. See Section 11.4 [Bell], page 50.

C-a h   (hardcopy)
             Write a hardcopy of the current window to the file "hardcopy.*n*".   See
             Section 18.1 [Hardcopy], page 77.

C-a H   (log)
             Toggle logging of the current window to the file "screenlog.*n*". See Section 18.2
             [Log], page 77.

C-a i
C-a C-i   (info)
             Show info about the current window. See Section 11.6 [Info], page 50.

C-a k
C-a C-k   (kill)
             Destroy the current window. See Section 10.3 [Kill], page 41.

C-a l
C-a C-l   (redisplay)
             Fully refresh the current window. See Section 11.7 [Redisplay], page 51.

C-a L   (login)
             Toggle the current window's login state. See Section 10.4 [Login], page 41.

C-a m
C-a C-m   (lastmsg)
             Repeat the last message displayed in the message line. See Section 17.3 [Last
             Message], page 75.

`C-a M`   (monitor) Toggle monitoring of the current window. See Section 10.6 [Monitor], page 42.

`C-a SPC`
`C-a n`
`C-a C-n`   (next)
                   Switch to the next window. See Chapter 7 [Selecting], page 29.

`C-a N`   (number)
                   Show the number (and title) of the current window. See Section 20.7 [Number], page 83.

`C-a p`
`C-a C-p`
`C-a C-h`
`C-a BACKSPACE`
                   (prev)
                   Switch to the previous window (opposite of `C-a n`). See Chapter 7 [Selecting], page 29.

`C-a q`
`C-a C-q`   (xon)
                   Send a ^Q (ASCII XON) to the current window. See Section 15.3 [XON/XOFF], page 68.

`C-a Q`   (only)
                   Delete all regions but the current one. See Chapter 9 [Regions], page 37.

`C-a r`
`C-a C-r`   (wrap)
                   Toggle the current window's line-wrap setting (turn the current window's automatic margins on or off). See Section 11.8 [Wrap], page 52.

`C-a s`
`C-a C-s`   (xoff)
                   Send a ^S (ASCII XOFF) to the current window. See Section 15.3 [XON/XOFF], page 68.

`C-a S`   (split)
                   Split the current region into two new ones. See Chapter 9 [Regions], page 37.

`C-a t`
`C-a C-t`   (time)
                   Show the load average and xref. See Section 20.9 [Time], page 83.

`C-a v`   (version)
                   Display the version and compilation date. See Section 20.11 [Version], page 84.

`C-a C-v`   (digraph)
                   Enter digraph. See Section 11.3 [Digraph], page 49.

`C-a w`
`C-a C-w`   (windows)
                   Show a list of active windows. See Section 10.7 [Windows], page 42.

`C-a W`   (width)
              Toggle between 80 and 132 columns. See Section 11.10 [Window Size], page 52.

`C-a x`
`C-a C-x`   (lockscreen)
              Lock your terminal. See Section 8.3 [Lock], page 32.

`C-a X`   (remove)
              Kill the current region. See Chapter 9 [Regions], page 37.

`C-a z`
`C-a C-z`   (suspend)
              Suspend **screen**. See Section 8.6 [Suspend], page 35.

`C-a Z`   (reset)
              Reset the virtual terminal to its "power-on" values. See Section 11.9 [Reset],
              page 52.

`C-a .`   (dumptermcap)
              Write out a '`.termcap`' file. See Section 16.2 [Dump Termcap], page 70.

`C-a ?`   (help)
              Show key bindings. See Section 14.4 [Help], page 64.

`C-a C-\`   (quit)
              Kill all windows and terminate **screen**. See Section 8.7 [Quit], page 35.

`C-a :`   (colon)
              Enter a command line. See Section 4.3 [Colon], page 9.

`C-a [`
`C-a C-[`
`C-a ESC`   (copy)
              Enter copy/scrollback mode. See Section 12.1 [Copy], page 55.

`C-a ]`
`C-a C-]`   (paste .)
              Write the contents of the paste buffer to the stdin queue of the current window.
              See Section 12.2 [Paste], page 57.

`C-a {`
`C-a }`   (history)
              Copy and paste a previous (command) line. See Section 12.5 [History], page 59.

`C-a >`   (writebuf)
              Write the paste buffer out to the screen-exchange file. See Section 12.4 [Screen
              Exchange], page 59.

`C-a <`   (readbuf)
              Read the screen-exchange file into the paste buffer. See Section 12.4 [Screen
              Exchange], page 59.

`C-a =`   (removebuf)
              Delete the screen-exchange file. See Section 12.4 [Screen Exchange], page 59.

`C-a _`   (silence)
             Start/stop monitoring the current window for inactivity. See Section 20.8 [Silence], page 83,

`C-a ,`   (license)
             Show the copyright page.

`C-a *`   (displays)
             Show the listing of attached displays.

5.2 Command Summary

`acladd usernames`
             Allow other users in this session. See Section 8.4 [Multiuser Session], page 32.

`aclchg usernames permbits list`
             Change a user's permissions. See Section 8.4 [Multiuser Session], page 32.

`acldel username`
             Disallow other user in this session. See Section 8.4 [Multiuser Session], page 32.

`aclgrp usrname [groupname]`
             Inherit permissions granted to a group leader. See Section 8.4 [Multiuser Session], page 32.

`aclumask [users]+/-bits ...`
             Predefine access to new windows. See Section 8.4.7 [Umask], page 33.

`activity message`
             Set the activity notification message. See Section 10.6 [Monitor], page 42.

`addacl usernames`
             Synonym to `acladd`. See Section 8.4 [Multiuser Session], page 32.

`allpartial state`
             Set all windows to partial refresh. See Section 11.7 [Redisplay], page 51.

`altscreen state`
             Enables support for the "alternate screen" terminal capability. See Section 11.7 [Redisplay], page 51.

`at [ident][#|*|%] command [args]`
             Execute a command at other displays or windows. See Section 20.1 [At], page 81.

`attrcolor attrib [attribute/color-modifier]`
             Map attributes to colors. See Section 20.15 [Attrcolor], page 85.

`autodetach state`
             Automatically detach the session on SIGHUP. See Section 8.1 [Detach], page 31.

`autonuke state`
             Enable a clear screen to discard unwritten output. See Section 16.6 [Autonuke], page 73.

backtick *id lifespan autorefresh command* [*args*]
>   Define a command for the backtick string escape. See Section 20.19 [Backtick], page 86.

bce [*state*]
>   Change background color erase. See Section 11.11 [Character Processing], page 52.

bell_msg [*message*]
>   Set the bell notification message. See Section 11.4 [Bell], page 50.

bind [-c *class*] *key* [*command* [*args*]]
>   Bind a command to a key. See Section 14.1 [Bind], page 63.

bindkey [*opts*] [*string* [*cmd args*]]
>   Bind a string to a series of keystrokes. See Section 14.5 [Bindkey], page 64.

blanker   Blank the screen. See Section 20.20 [Screen Saver], page 86.

blankerprg
>   Define a blanker program. See Section 20.20 [Screen Saver], page 86.

break [*duration*]
>   Send a break signal to the current window. See Section 20.2 [Break], page 81.

breaktype [*tcsendbreak* | *TCSBRK* | *TIOCSBRK*]
>   Specify how to generate breaks. See Section 20.2 [Break], page 81.

bufferfile [*exchange-file*]
>   Select a file for screen-exchange. See Section 12.4 [Screen Exchange], page 59.

c1 [*state*]
>   Change c1 code processing. See Section 11.11 [Character Processing], page 52.

caption *mode* [*string*]
>   Change caption mode and string. See Chapter 9 [Regions], page 37.

chacl *usernames permbits list*
>   Synonym to **aclchg**. See Section 8.4 [Multiuser Session], page 32.

charset *set*
>   Change character set slot designation. See Section 11.11 [Character Processing], page 52.

chdir [*directory*]
>   Change the current directory for future windows. See Section 6.1 [Chdir], page 25.

clear   Clear the window screen. See Section 11.5 [Clear], page 50.

colon   Enter a **screen** command. See Section 4.3 [Colon], page 9.

command [-c *class*]
>   Simulate the screen escape key. See Section 14.3 [Command Character], page 64.

`compacthist [`*`state`*`]`
>   Selects compaction of trailing empty lines. See Section 12.1.2 [Scrollback], page 55.

`console [`*`state`*`]`
>   Grab or ungrab console output. See Section 10.2 [Console], page 41.

`copy`   Enter copy mode. See Section 12.1 [Copy], page 55.

`copy_reg [`*`key`*`]`
>   Removed. Use **paste** instead. See Section 12.3 [Registers], page 58.

`crlf` *`state`*
>   Select line break behavior for copying. See Section 12.1.1 [Line Termination], page 55.

`debug` *`state`*
>   Suppress/allow debugging output. See Section 20.3 [Debug], page 82.

`defautonuke` *`state`*
>   Select default autonuke behavior. See Section 16.6 [Autonuke], page 73.

`defbce` *`state`*
>   Select background color erase. See Section 11.11 [Character Processing], page 52.

`defbreaktype [`*`tcsendbreak`* `|` *`TCSBRK`* `|` *`TIOCSBRK`*`]`
>   Specify the default for generating breaks. See Section 20.2 [Break], page 81.

`defc1` *`state`*
>   Select default c1 processing behavior. See Section 11.11 [Character Processing], page 52.

`defcharset [`*`set`*`]`
>   Change defaul character set slot designation. See Section 11.11 [Character Processing], page 52.

`defencoding` *`enc`*
>   Select default window encoding. See Section 11.11 [Character Processing], page 52.

`defescape` *`xy`*
>   Set the default command and **meta** characters. See Section 14.3 [Command Character], page 64.

`defflow` *`fstate`*
>   Select default flow control behavior. See Section 15.2 [Flow], page 67.

`defgr` *`state`*
>   Select default GR processing behavior. See Section 11.11 [Character Processing], page 52.

`defhstatus [`*`status`*`]`
>   Select default window hardstatus line. See Section 10.8 [Hardstatus], page 43.

`deflog` *`state`*
>   Select default window logging behavior. See Section 18.2 [Log], page 77.

`deflogin` *state*
> Select default utmp logging behavior. See Section 10.4 [Login], page 41.

`defmode` *mode*
> Select default file mode for ptys. See Section 10.5 [Mode], page 41.

`defmonitor` *state*
> Select default activity monitoring behavior. See Section 10.6 [Monitor], page 42.

`defnonblock` *state|numsecs*
> Select default nonblock mode. See Section 20.6 [Nonblock], page 82.

`defobuflimit` *limit*
> Select default output buffer limit. See Section 16.7 [Obuflimit], page 73.

`defscrollback` *num*
> Set default lines of scrollback. See Section 12.1.2 [Scrollback], page 55.

`defshell` *command*
> Set the default program for new windows. See Section 6.4 [Shell], page 26.

`defsilence` *state*
> Select default idle monitoring behavior. See Section 20.8 [Silence], page 83.

`defslowpaste` *msec*
> Select the default inter-character timeout when pasting. See Section 12.2 [Paste], page 57.

`defutf8` *state*
> Select default character encoding. See Section 11.11 [Character Processing], page 52.

`defwrap` *state*
> Set default line-wrapping behavior. See Section 11.8 [Wrap], page 52.

`defwritelock` *on|off|auto*
> Set default writelock behavior. See Section 8.4 [Multiuser Session], page 32.

`defzombie` *[keys]*
> Keep dead windows. See Section 20.12 [Zombie], page 84.

`detach [-h]`
> Disconnect **screen** from the terminal. See Section 8.1 [Detach], page 31.

`digraph`   Enter digraph sequence. See Section 11.3 [Digraph], page 49.

`dinfo`   Display terminal information. See Section 11.6 [Info], page 50.

`displays`   List currently active user interfaces. See Section 8.4.6 [Displays], page 33.

`dumptermcap`
> Write the window's termcap entry to a file. See Section 16.2 [Dump Termcap], page 70.

`echo [-n]` *message*
> Display a message on startup. See Chapter 19 [Startup], page 79.

encoding *enc* [*denc*]

        Set the encoding of a window. See Section 11.11 [Character Processing], page 52.

escape *xy*

        Set the command and **meta** characters. See Section 14.3 [Command Character], page 64.

eval *command1* [*command2* ...]

        Parse and execute each argument. See Section 20.17 [Eval], page 85.

exec [[*fdpat*] *command* [*args* ...]]

        Run a subprocess (filter). See Section 13.1 [Exec], page 61.

fit   Change window size to current display size. See Section 11.10 [Window Size], page 52.

flow [*fstate*]

        Set flow control behavior. See Section 15.2 [Flow], page 67.

focus   Move focus to next region. See Chapter 9 [Regions], page 37.

gr [*state*]

        Change GR charset processing. See Section 11.11 [Character Processing], page 52.

hardcopy [-h] [*file*]

        Write out the contents of the current window. See Section 18.1 [Hardcopy], page 77.

hardcopy_append *state*

        Append to hardcopy files. See Section 18.1 [Hardcopy], page 77.

hardcopydir *directory*

        Place, where to dump hardcopy files. See Section 18.1 [Hardcopy], page 77.

hardstatus [*state*]

        Use the hardware status line. See Section 17.2 [Hardware Status Line], page 75.

height [*lines* [*cols*]]

        Set display height. See Section 11.10 [Window Size], page 52.

help [-c *class*]

        Display current key bindings. See Section 14.4 [Help], page 64.

history   Find previous command beginning .... See Section 12.5 [History], page 59.

hstatus *status*

        Change the window's hardstatus line. See Section 10.8 [Hardstatus], page 43.

idle [*timeout* [*cmd args*]]

        Define a screen saver command. See Section 20.20 [Screen Saver], page 86.

ignorecase [*state*]

        Ignore character case in searches. See Section 12.1.7 [Searching], page 56.

info   Display window settings. See Section 11.6 [Info], page 50.

`ins_reg [key]`
          Removed, use **paste** instead. See Section 12.3 [Registers], page 58.

`kill`   Destroy the current window. See Section 10.3 [Kill], page 41.

`lastmsg`   Redisplay the last message. See Section 17.3 [Last Message], page 75.

`license`   Display licensing information. See Chapter 19 [Startup], page 79.

`lockscreen`
          Lock the controlling terminal. See Section 8.3 [Lock], page 32.

`log [state]`
          Log all output in the current window. See Section 18.2 [Log], page 77.

`logfile filename`
          Place where to collect logfiles. See Section 18.2 [Log], page 77.

`login [state]`
          Log the window in '/etc/utmp'. See Section 10.4 [Login], page 41.

`logtstamp [state]`
          Configure logfile time-stamps. See Section 18.2 [Log], page 77.

`mapdefault`
          Use only the default mapping table for the next keystroke. See Section 14.7 [Bindkey Control], page 65.

`mapnotnext`
          Don't try to do keymapping on the next keystroke. See Section 14.7 [Bindkey Control], page 65.

`maptimeout timo`
          Set the inter-character timeout used for keymapping. See Section 14.7 [Bindkey Control], page 65.

`markkeys string`
          Rebind keys in copy mode. See Section 12.1.3 [Copy Mode Keys], page 55.

`maxwin n`   Set the maximum window number. See Section 20.18 [Maxwin], page 86.

`meta`   Insert the command character. See Section 14.3 [Command Character], page 64.

`monitor [state]`
          Monitor activity in window. See Section 10.6 [Monitor], page 42.

`msgminwait sec`
          Set minimum message wait. See Section 17.4 [Message Wait], page 76.

`msgwait sec`
          Set default message wait. See Section 17.4 [Message Wait], page 76.

`multiuser state`
          Go into single or multi user mode. See Section 8.4 [Multiuser Session], page 32.

`nethack state`
          Use **nethack**-like error messages. See Section 20.5 [Nethack], page 82.

next   Switch to the next window. See Chapter 7 [Selecting], page 29.

nonblock [*state*|*numsecs*]
              Disable flow control to the current display. See Section 20.6 [Nonblock],
              page 82.|*numsecs*]

number [*n*]
              Change/display the current window's number. See Section 20.7 [Number],
              page 83.

obuflimit [*limit*]
              Select output buffer limit. See Section 16.7 [Obuflimit], page 73.

only   Kill all other regions. See Chapter 9 [Regions], page 37.

other   Switch to the window you were in last. See Chapter 7 [Selecting], page 29.

partial *state*
              Set window to partial refresh. See Section 11.7 [Redisplay], page 51.

password [*crypted_pw*]
              Set reattach password. See Section 8.1 [Detach], page 31.

paste [*src_regs* [*dest_reg*]]
              Paste contents of paste buffer or registers somewhere. See Section 12.2 [Paste],
              page 57.

pastefont [*state*]
              Include font information in the paste buffer. See Section 12.2 [Paste], page 57.

pow_break
              Close and Reopen the window's terminal. See Section 20.2 [Break], page 81.

pow_detach
              Detach and hang up. See Section 8.2 [Power Detach], page 31.

pow_detach_msg [*message*]
              Set message displayed on **pow_detach**. See Section 8.2 [Power Detach], page 31.

prev   Switch to the previous window. See Chapter 7 [Selecting], page 29.

printcmd [*cmd*]
              Set a command for VT100 printer port emulation. See Section 20.13 [Printcmd],
              page 84.

process [*key*]
              Treat a register as input to **screen**. See Section 12.3 [Registers], page 58.

quit   Kill all windows and exit. See Section 8.7 [Quit], page 35.

readbuf [-e *encoding*] [*filename*]
              Read the paste buffer from the screen-exchange file. See Section 12.4 [Screen
              Exchange], page 59.

readreg [-e *encoding*] [*reg* [*file*]]
              Load a register from paste buffer or file. See Section 12.3 [Registers], page 58.

redisplay
          Redisplay the current window. See Section 11.7 [Redisplay], page 51.

register [-e *encoding*] *key string*
          Store a string to a register. See Section 12.3 [Registers], page 58.

remove   Kill current region. See Chapter 9 [Regions], page 37.

removebuf
          Delete the screen-exchange file. See Section 12.4 [Screen Exchange], page 59.

reset   Reset the terminal settings for the window. See Section 11.9 [Reset], page 52.

resize [(+/-)lines]
          Grow or shrink a region

screen [*opts*] [*n*] [*cmd* [*args*]]
          Create a new window. See Section 6.2 [Screen Command], page 25.

scrollback *num*
          Set size of scrollback buffer. See Section 12.1.2 [Scrollback], page 55.

select [*n*]
          Switch to a specified window. See Chapter 7 [Selecting], page 29.

sessionname [*name*]
          Name this session. See Section 8.5 [Session Name], page 34.

setenv [*var* [*string*]]
          Set an environment variable for new windows. See Section 6.3 [Setenv], page 26.

setsid *state*
          Controll process group creation for windows. See Section 20.16 [Setsid], page 85.

shell *command*
          Set the default program for new windows. See Section 6.4 [Shell], page 26.

shelltitle *title*
          Set the default name for new windows. See Section 6.4 [Shell], page 26.

silence [*state*|*seconds*]
          Monitor a window for inactivity. See Section 20.8 [Silence], page 83.

silencewait *seconds*
          Default timeout to trigger an inactivity notify. See Section 20.8 [Silence],
          page 83.

sleep *num*
          Pause during startup. See Chapter 19 [Startup], page 79.

slowpaste *msec*
          Slow down pasting in windows. See Section 12.2 [Paste], page 57.

source *file*
          Run commands from a file. See Section 4.2 [Source], page 9.

sorendition [*attr* [*color*]]
          Change text highlighting. See Section 20.14 [Sorendition], page 85.

`split`   Split region into two parts. See Chapter 9 [Regions], page 37.

`startup_message` *state*

Display copyright notice on startup. See Chapter 19 [Startup], page 79.

`stuff` *string*

Stuff a string in the input buffer of a window. See Section 12.2 [Paste], page 57.

`su [`*username* `[`*password* `[`*password2*`]]]`

Identify a user. See Section 8.4 [Multiuser Session], page 32.

`suspend`   Put session in background. See Section 8.6 [Suspend], page 35.

`term` *term*

Set $TERM for new windows. See Section 6.5 [Term], page 26.

`termcap` *term terminal-tweaks* `[`*window-tweaks*`]`

Tweak termcap entries for best performance. See Section 16.3 [Termcap Syntax], page 70.

`terminfo` *term terminal-tweaks* `[`*window-tweaks*`]`

Ditto, for terminfo systems. See Section 16.3 [Termcap Syntax], page 70.

`termcapinfo` *term terminal-tweaks* `[`*window-tweaks*`]`

Ditto, for both systems. See Section 16.3 [Termcap Syntax], page 70.

`time [`*string*`]`

Display time and load average. See Section 20.9 [Time], page 83.

`title [`*windowtitle*`]`

Set the name of the current window. See Section 10.1.1 [Title Command], page 39.

`umask [`*users*`]+/-`*bits* ...

Synonym to `aclumask`. See Section 8.4.7 [Umask], page 33.

`unsetenv` *var*

Unset environment variable for new windows. See Section 6.3 [Setenv], page 26.

`utf8 [`*state* `[`*dstate*`]]`

Select character encoding of the current window. See Section 11.11 [Character Processing], page 52.

`vbell [`*state*`]`

Use visual bell. See Section 11.4 [Bell], page 50.

`vbell_msg [`*message*`]`

Set vbell message. See Section 11.4 [Bell], page 50.

`vbellwait` *sec*

Set delay for vbell message. See Section 11.4 [Bell], page 50.

`version`   Display `screen` version. See Section 20.11 [Version], page 84.

`wall` *message*

Write a message to all displays. See Section 8.4 [Multiuser Session], page 32.

`width [cols [lines]]`
> Set the width of the window. See Section 11.10 [Window Size], page 52.

`windowlist [-b] | string [string] | title [title]`
> Present a list of all windows for selection. See Section 7.4 [Windowlist], page 29.

`windows`   List active windows. See Section 10.7 [Windows], page 42.

`wrap [state]`
> Control line-wrap behavior. See Section 11.8 [Wrap], page 52.

`writebuf [-e encoding] [filename]`
> Write paste buffer to screen-exchange file. See Section 12.4 [Screen Exchange], page 59.

`writelock on|off|auto`
> Grant exclusive write permission. See Section 8.4 [Multiuser Session], page 32.

`xoff`   Send an XOFF character. See Section 15.3 [XON/XOFF], page 68.

`xon`   Send an XON character. See Section 15.3 [XON/XOFF], page 68.

`zmodem [off|auto|catch|pass]`
> Define how screen treats zmodem requests. See Section 20.21 [Zmodem], page 87.

`zombie [keys [onerror] ]`
> Keep dead windows. See Section 20.12 [Zombie], page 84.

6 New Window

This section describes the commands for creating a new window for running programs. When a new window is created, the first available number from the range 0...9 is assigned to it. The number of windows is limited at compile-time by the MAXWIN configuration parameter.

6.1 Chdir

chdir [*directory*]   [Command]
> (none)
> Change the current directory of **screen** to the specified directory or, if called without an argument, to your home directory (the value of the environment variable $HOME). All windows that are created by means of the **screen** command from within '.screenrc' or by means of *C-a : screen ...* or *C-a c* use this as their default directory. Without a **chdir** command, this would be the directory from which **screen** was invoked. Hardcopy and log files are always written to the *window's* default directory, *not* the current directory of the process running in the window. You can use this command multiple times in your '.screenrc' to start various windows in different default directories, but the last **chdir** value will affect all the windows you create interactively.

6.2 Screen Command

screen [*opts*] [*n*] [*cmd* [*args*]]   [Command]
> (*C-a c, C-a C-c*)
> Establish a new window. The flow-control options ('-f', '-fn' and '-fa'), title option ('-t'), login options ('-l' and '-ln') , terminal type option ('-T *term*'), the all-capability-flag ('-a') and scrollback option ('-h *num*') may be specified with each command. The option ('-M') turns monitoring on for this window. The option ('-L') turns output logging on for this window. If an optional number *n* in the range 0...9 is given, the window number *n* is assigned to the newly created window (or, if this number is already in-use, the next available number). If a command is specified after **screen**, this command (with the given arguments) is started in the window; otherwise, a shell is created.
>
> Screen has built in some functionality of 'cu' and 'telnet'. See Section 6.6 [Window Types], page 26.

Thus, if your '.screenrc' contains the lines

```
# example for .screenrc:
screen 1
screen -fn -t foobar 2 -L telnet foobar
```

screen creates a shell window (in window #1) and a window with a TELNET connection to the machine foobar (with no flow-control using the title 'foobar' in window #2) and will write a logfile 'screenlog.2' of the telnet session. If you do not include any **screen** commands in your '.screenrc' file, then **screen** defaults to creating a single shell window, number zero. When the initialization is completed, **screen** switches to the last window specified in your .screenrc file or, if none, it opens default window #0.

6.3 Setenv

setenv *var string*   [Command]
> (none)
> Set the environment variable *var* to value *string*. If only *var* is specified, the user will be prompted to enter a value. If no parameters are specified, the user will be prompted for both variable and value. The environment is inherited by all subsequently forked shells.

unsetenv *var*   [Command]
> (none)
> Unset an environment variable.

6.4 Shell

shell *command*   [Command]
defshell *command*   [Command]
> (none)
> Set the command to be used to create a new shell. This overrides the value of the environment variable $SHELL. This is useful if you'd like to run a tty-enhancer which is expecting to execute the program specified in $SHELL. If the command begins with a '-' character, the shell will be started as a login-shell.
>
> **defshell** is currently a synonym to the **shell** command.

shelltitle *title*   [Command]
> (none)
> Set the title for all shells created during startup or by the C-a C-c command. See Section 10.1 [Naming Windows], page 39, for details about what titles are.

6.5 Term

term *term*   [Command]
> (none)
> In each window **screen** opens, it sets the $TERM variable to **screen** by default, unless no description for **screen** is installed in the local termcap or terminfo data base. In that case it pretends that the terminal emulator is 'vt100'. This won't do much harm, as **screen** is VT100/ANSI compatible. The use of the **term** command is discouraged for non-default purpose. That is, one may want to specify special $TERM settings (e.g. vt100) for the next **screen rlogin othermachine** command. Use the command **screen -T vt100 rlogin othermachine** rather than setting and resetting the default.

6.6 Window Types

Screen provides three different window types. New windows are created with **screen**'s 'screen' command (see Section 6.2 [Screen Command], page 25). The first parameter to the 'screen' command defines which type of window is created. The different window types are all special cases of the normal type. They have been added in order to allow screen to be used efficiently as a console with 100 or more windows.

- The normal window contains a shell (default, if no parameter is given) or any other system command that could be executed from a shell. (e.g. 'slogin', etc...).

- If a tty (character special device) name (e.g. '/dev/ttya') is specified as the first parameter, then the window is directly connected to this device. This window type is similar to 'screen cu -l /dev/ttya'. Read and write access is required on the device node, an exclusive open is attempted on the node to mark the connection line as busy. An optional parameter is allowed consisting of a comma separated list of flags in the notation used by 'stty(1)':

<baud_rate>
Usually 300, 1200, 9600 or 19200. This affects transmission as well as receive speed.

cs8 or cs7
Specify the transmission of eight (or seven) bits per byte.

ixon or -ixon
Enables (or disables) software flow-control (CTRL-S/CTRL-Q) for sending data.

ixoff or -ixoff
Enables (or disables) software flow-control for receiving data.

istrip or -istrip
Clear (or keep) the eight bit in each received byte.

You may want to specify as many of these options as applicable. Unspecified options cause the terminal driver to make up the parameter values of the connection. These values are system-dependent and may be in defaults or values saved from a previous connection.

For tty windows, the info command shows some of the modem control lines in the status line. These may include 'RTS', 'CTS', 'DTR', 'CD' and more. This depends rather on on the available ioctl()'s and system header files than on the physical capabilities of the serial board. The name of a logical low (inactive) signal is preceded by an exclamation mark ('!'), otherwise the signal is logical high (active). Unsupported but shown signals are usually shown low. When the CLOCAL status bit is true, the whole set of modem signals is placed inside curly braces ('{' and '}'). When the CRTSCTS or TIOCSOFTCAR bit is true, the signals 'CTS' or 'CD' are shown in parenthesis, respectively.

For tty windows, the command break causes the Data transmission line (TxD) to go low for a specified period of time. This is expected to be interpreted as break signal on the other side. No data is sent and no modem control line is changed when a break is issued.

- If the first parameter is //telnet, the second parameter is expected to be a host name, and an optional third parameter may specify a TCP port number (default decimal 23). Screen will connect to a server listening on the remote host and use the telnet protocol to communicate with that server.

For telnet windows, the command **info** shows details about the connection in square brackets ('[' and ']') at the end of the status line.

b   BINARY. The connection is in binary mode.

e   ECHO. Local echo is disabled.

c   SGA. The connection is in 'character mode' (default: 'line mode').

t   TTYPE. The terminal type has been requested by the remote host. Screen sends the name **screen** unless instructed otherwise (see also the command 'term').

w   NAWS. The remote site is notified about window size changes.

f   LFLOW. The remote host will send flow control information. (Ignored at the moment.)

Additional flags for debugging are 'x', 't' and 'n' (XDISPLOC, TSPEED and NEWENV).

For telnet windows, the command **break** sends the telnet code **IAC BREAK** (decimal 243) to the remote host.

7 Selecting a Window

This section describes the commands for switching between windows in an **screen** session. The windows are numbered from 0 to 9, and are created in that order by default (see Chapter 6 [New Window], page 25).

7.1 Moving Back and Forth

next   [Command]
> (*C-a SPC, C-a n, C-a C-n*)
> Switch to the next window. This command can be used repeatedly to cycle through the list of windows. (On some terminals, C-SPC generates a NUL character, so you must release the control key before pressing space.)

prev   [Command]
> (*C-a p, C-a C-p*)
> Switch to the previous window (the opposite of *C-a n*).

7.2 Other Window

other   [Command]
> (*C-a C-a*)
> Switch to the last window displayed. Note that this command defaults to the command character typed twice, unless overridden. For instance, if you use the option '-e]x', this command becomes *]]* (see Section 14.3 [Command Character], page 64).

7.3 Select

select [*n*]   [Command]
> (*C-a n, C-a '*)
> Switch to the window with the number *n*. If no window number is specified, you get prompted for an identifier. This can be a window name (title) or a number. When a new window is established, the lowest available number is assigned to this window. Thus, the first window can be activated by **select 0**; there can be no more than 10 windows present simultaneously (unless screen is compiled with a higher MAXWIN setting). There are two special arguments, **select -** switches to the internal blank window and **select .** switches to the current window. The latter is useful if used with screen's **-X** option.

7.4 Windowlist

windowlist [*-b*] [*-m*]   [Command]
windowlist *string* [**string**]   [Command]
windowlist *title* [**title**]   [Command]
> (*C-a "*)
> Display all windows in a table for visual window selection. The desired window can be selected via the standard movement keys (see Section 12.1.4 [Movement], page 56) and

activated via the return key. If the **-b** option is given, screen will switch to the blank window before presenting the list, so that the current window is also selectable. The **-m** option changes the order of the windows, instead of sorting by window numbers screen uses its internal most-recently-used list.

The table format can be changed with the string and title option, the title is displayed as table heading, while the lines are made by using the string setting. The default setting is 'Num Name%=Flags' for the title and '%3n %t%=%f' for the lines. See the string escapes chapter (see Chapter 21 [String Escapes], page 89) for more codes (e.g. color settings).

8 Session Management Commands

Perhaps the most useful feature of **screen** is the way it allows the user to move a session between terminals, by detaching and reattaching. This also makes life easier for modem users who have to deal with unexpected loss of carrier.

8.1 Detach

autodetach *state*   [Command]

> (none)
> Sets whether **screen** will automatically detach upon hangup, which saves all your running programs until they are resumed with a **screen -r** command. When turned off, a hangup signal will terminate **screen** and all the processes it contains. Autodetach is on by default.

detach   [Command]

> (*C-a d, C-a C-d*)
> Detach the **screen** session (disconnect it from the terminal and put it into the background). A detached **screen** can be resumed by invoking **screen** with the **-r** option (see Chapter 3 [Invoking Screen], page 5). The **-h** option tells screen to immediately close the connection to the terminal ('**hangup**').

password [*crypted_pw*]   [Command]

> (none)
> Present a crypted password in your '.**screenrc**' file and screen will ask for it, whenever someone attempts to resume a detached session. This is useful, if you have privileged programs running under **screen** and you want to protect your session from reattach attempts by users that managed to assume your uid. (I.e. any superuser.) If no crypted password is specified, screen prompts twice a password and places its encryption in the paste buffer. Default is 'none', which disables password checking.

8.2 Power Detach

pow_detach   [Command]

> (*C-a D D*)
> Mainly the same as **detach**, but also sends a HANGUP signal to the parent process of **screen**.
> *Caution*: This will result in a logout if **screen** was started from your login shell.

pow_detach_msg [*message*]   [Command]

> (none)
> The *message* specified here is output whenever a power detach is performed. It may be used as a replacement for a logout message or to reset baud rate, etc. Without parameter, the current message is shown.

8.3 Lock

lockscreen   [Command]

> (*C-a x*, *C-a C-x*)
> Call a screenlock program ('/local/bin/lck' or '/usr/bin/lock' or a builtin, if no
> other is available). Screen does not accept any command keys until this program
> terminates. Meanwhile processes in the windows may continue, as the windows are in
> the detached state. The screenlock program may be changed through the environment
> variable $LOCKPRG (which must be set in the shell from which screen is started) and
> is executed with the user's uid and gid.
>
> Warning: When you leave other shells unlocked and have no password set on screen,
> the lock is void: One could easily re-attach from an unlocked shell. This feature
> should rather be called lockterminal.

8.4 Multiuser Session

These commands allow other users to gain access to one single screen session. When
attaching to a multiuser screen the sessionname is specified as username/sessionname to
the -S command line option. Screen must be compiled with multiuser support to enable
features described here.

8.4.1 Multiuser

multiuser *state*   [Command]

> (none)
> Switch between single-user and multi-user mode. Standard screen operation is single-
> user. In multi-user mode the commands acladd, aclchg and acldel can be used to
> enable (and disable) other users accessing this screen.

8.4.2 Acladd

acladd *usernames*   [Command]
addacl *usernames*   [Command]

> (none)
> Enable users to fully access this screen session. *Usernames* can be one user or a
> comma separated list of users. This command enables to attach to the screen session
> and performs the equivalent of aclchg *usernames* +rwx "#?". To add a user with
> restricted access, use the aclchg command below. Addacl is a synonym to acladd.
> Multi-user mode only.

8.4.3 Aclchg

aclchg *usernames permbits list*   [Command]
chacl *usernames permbits list*   [Command]

> (none)
> Change permissions for a comma separated list of users. Permission bits are repre-
> sented as 'r', 'w' and 'x'. Prefixing '+' grants the permission, '-' removes it. The
> third parameter is a comma separated list of commands or windows (specified either

by number or title). The special list '#' refers to all windows, '?' to all commands. If *usernames* consists of a single '*', all known users are affected. A command can be executed when the user has the 'x' bit for it. The user can type input to a window when he has its 'w' bit set and no other user obtains a writelock for this window. Other bits are currently ignored. To withdraw the writelock from another user in e.g. window 2: 'aclchg *username* -w+w 2'. To allow read-only access to the session: 'aclchg *username* -w "#"'. As soon as a user's name is known to screen, he can attach to the session and (per default) has full permissions for all command and windows. Execution permission for the acl commands, at and others should also be removed or the user may be able to regain write permission. Chacl is a synonym to aclchg. Multi-user mode only.

8.4.4 Acldel

acldel *username*   [Command]
> (none)
> Remove a user from screen's access control list. If currently attached, all the user's displays are detached from the session. He cannot attach again. Multi-user mode only.

8.4.5 Aclgrp

aclgrp *username* [*groupname*]   [Command]
> (none)
> Creates groups of users that share common access rights. The name of the group is the username of the group leader. Each member of the group inherits the permissions that are granted to the group leader. That means, if a user fails an access check, another check is made for the group leader. A user is removed from all groups the special value 'none' is used for *groupname*. If the second parameter is omitted all groups the user is in are listed.

8.4.6 Displays

displays   [Command]
> (*C-a **)
> Shows a tabular listing of all currently connected user front-ends (displays). This is most useful for multiuser sessions.

8.4.7 aclumask

aclumask [*users*]+/-*bits* ...   [Command]
umask [*users*]+/-*bits* ...   [Command]
> (none)
> This specifies the access other users have to windows that will be created by the caller of the command. *Users* may be no, one or a comma separated list of known usernames. If no users are specified, a list of all currently known users is assumed. *Bits* is any combination of access control bits allowed defined with the aclchg command. The special username '?' predefines the access that not yet known users will be granted to any window initially. The special username '??' predefines the access that not yet

known users are granted to any command. Rights of the special username nobody cannot be changed (see the `su` command). `Umask` is a synonym to `aclumask`.

8.4.8 Wall

`wall message`   [Command]
> (none)
> Write a message to all displays. The message will appear in the terminal's status line.

8.4.9 Writelock

`writelock on|off|auto`   [Command]
> (none)
> In addition to access control lists, not all users may be able to write to the same window at once. Per default, writelock is in 'auto' mode and grants exclusive input permission to the user who is the first to switch to the particular window. When he leaves the window, other users may obtain the writelock (automatically). The writelock of the current window is disabled by the command `writelock off`. If the user issues the command `writelock on` he keeps the exclusive write permission while switching to other windows.

`defwritelock on|off|auto`   [Command]
> (none)
> Sets the default writelock behavior for new windows. Initially all windows will be created with no writelocks.

8.4.10 Su

`su [username [password [password2]]]`   [Command]
> (none)
> Substitute the user of a display. The command prompts for all parameters that are omitted. If passwords are specified as parameters, they have to be specified uncrypted. The first password is matched against the systems passwd database, the second password is matched against the `screen` password as set with the commands `acladd` or `password`. Su may be useful for the `screen` administrator to test multiuser setups. When the identification fails, the user has access to the commands available for user 'nobody'. These are `detach`, `license`, `version`, `help` and `displays`.

8.5 Session Name

`sessionname [name]`   [Command]
> (none)
> Rename the current session. Note that for `screen -list` the name shows up with the process-id prepended. If the argument *name* is omitted, the name of this session is displayed.
> *Caution*: The `$STY` environment variable still reflects the old name. This may result in confusion. The default is constructed from the tty and host names.

8.6 Suspend

suspend   [Command]
>   (*C-a z*, *C-a C-z*)
>   Suspend **screen**. The windows are in the detached state while **screen** is suspended.
>   This feature relies on the parent shell being able to do job control.

8.7 Quit

quit   [Command]
>   (*C-a C-*)
>   Kill all windows and terminate **screen**. Note that on VT100-style terminals the keys
>   *C-4* and *C-* are identical. So be careful not to type *C-a C-4* when selecting window
>   no. 4. Use the empty bind command (as in **bind** "^\\") to remove a key binding (see
>   Chapter 14 [Key Binding], page 63).

9 Regions

Screen has the ability to display more than one window on the user's display. This is done by splitting the screen in regions, which can contain different windows.

9.1 Split

`split`   [Command]

> (`C-a S`)
> Split the current region into two new ones. All regions on the display are resized to make room for the new region. The blank window is displayed on the new region.

9.2 Focus

`focus`   [Command]

> (`C-a TAB`)
> Move the input focus to the next region. This is done in a cyclic way so that the top region is selected after the bottom one. If no subcommand is given it defaults to 'down'. 'up' cycles in the opposite order, 'top' and 'bottom' go to the top and bottom region respectively. Useful bindings are (j and k as in vi)

```
bind j focus down
bind k focus up
bind t focus top
bind b focus bottom
```

9.3 Only

`only`   [Command]

> (`C-a Q`)
> Kill all regions but the current one.

9.4 Remove

`remove`   [Command]

> (`C-a X`)
> Kill the current region. This is a no-op if there is only one region.

9.5 Resize

`resize [(+/-)lines]`   [Command]

> (none)
> Resize the current region. The space will be removed from or added to the region below or if there's not enough space from the region above.

```
resize +N      increase current region height by N
resize -N      decrease current region height by N
resize  N      set current region height to N
```

```
resize   =       make all windows equally high
resize   max     maximize current region height
resize   min     minimize current region height
```

9.6 Caption

caption always|splitonly [*string*]   [Command]
caption string [*string*]   [Command]
  (none)

  This command controls the display of the window captions. Normally a caption is
  only used if more than one window is shown on the display (split screen mode). But
  if the type is set to **always**, **screen** shows a caption even if only one window is
  displayed. The default is 'splitonly'.

  The second form changes the text used for the caption. You can use all string escapes
  (see Chapter 21 [String Escapes], page 89). **Screen** uses a default of '%3n %t'.

  You can mix both forms by providing the string as an additional argument.

9.7 Fit

fit   [Command]
  (*C-a F*)

  Change the window size to the size of the current region. This command is needed
  because screen doesn't adapt the window size automatically if the window is displayed
  more than once.

10 Window Settings

These commands control the way **screen** treats individual windows in a session. See Chapter 11 [Virtual Terminal], page 45, for commands to control the terminal emulation itself.

10.1 Naming Windows (Titles)

You can customize each window's name in the window display (viewed with the **windows** command (see Section 10.7 [Windows], page 42) by setting it with one of the title commands. Normally the name displayed is the actual command name of the program created in the window. However, it is sometimes useful to distinguish various programs of the same name or to change the name on-the-fly to reflect the current state of the window.

The default name for all shell windows can be set with the **shelltitle** command (see Section 6.4 [Shell], page 26). You can specify the name you want for a window with the '**-t**' option to the **screen** command when the window is created (see Section 6.2 [Screen Command], page 25). To change the name after the window has been created you can use the title-string escape-sequence (*ESC k name ESC *) and the **title** command (C-a A). The former can be output from an application to control the window's name under software control, and the latter will prompt for a name when typed. You can also bind predefined names to keys with the **title** command to set things quickly without prompting.

10.1.1 Title Command

title [*windowtitle*]   [Command]
  (*C-a A*)
  Set the name of the current window to *windowtitle*. If no name is specified, screen prompts for one.

10.1.2 Dynamic Titles

screen has a shell-specific heuristic that is enabled by setting the window's name to *search|name* and arranging to have a null title escape-sequence output as a part of your prompt. The *search* portion specifies an end-of-prompt search string, while the *name* portion specifies the default shell name for the window. If the *name* ends in a ':' **screen** will add what it believes to be the current command running in the window to the end of the specified name (e.g. *name:cmd*). Otherwise the current command name supersedes the shell name while it is running.

Here's how it works: you must modify your shell prompt to output a null title-escape-sequence (ESC k ESC \) as a part of your prompt. The last part of your prompt must be the same as the string you specified for the *search* portion of the title. Once this is set up, **screen** will use the title-escape-sequence to clear the previous command name and get ready for the next command. Then, when a newline is received from the shell, a search is made for the end of the prompt. If found, it will grab the first word after the matched string and use it as the command name. If the command name begins with '!', '%', or '^', **screen** will use the first word on the following line (if found) in preference to the just-found name. This helps csh users get more accurate titles when using job control or history recall commands.

10.1.3 Setting up your prompt for shell titles

One thing to keep in mind when adding a null title-escape-sequence to your prompt is that some shells (like the csh) count all the non-control characters as part of the prompt's length. If these invisible characters aren't a multiple of 8 then backspacing over a tab will result in an incorrect display. One way to get around this is to use a prompt like this:

```
set prompt='<ESC>[0000m<ESC>k<ESC>\% '
```

The escape-sequence '<ESC>[0000m' not only normalizes the character attributes, but all the zeros round the length of the invisible characters up to 8.

Tcsh handles escape codes in the prompt more intelligently, so you can specify your prompt like this:

```
set prompt="%{\ek\e\\%}\% "
```

Bash users will probably want to echo the escape sequence in the PROMPT_COMMAND:

```
PROMPT_COMMAND='printf "\033k\033\134"'
```

(I used '\134' to output a '\' because of a bug in v1.04).

10.1.4 Setting up shell titles in your '.screenrc'

Here are some .screenrc examples:

```
screen -t top 2 nice top
```

Adding this line to your .screenrc would start a niced version of the top command in window 2 named 'top' rather than 'nice'.

```
shelltitle '> |csh'
screen 1
```

This file would start a shell using the given shelltitle. The title specified is an auto-title that would expect the prompt and the typed command to look something like the following:

```
/usr/joe/src/dir> trn
```

(it looks after the '> ' for the command name). The window status would show the name 'trn' while the command was running, and revert to 'csh' upon completion.

```
bind R screen -t '% |root:' su
```

Having this command in your .screenrc would bind the key sequence *C-a R* to the su command and give it an auto-title name of 'root:'. For this auto-title to work, the screen could look something like this:

```
% !em
emacs file.c
```

Here the user typed the csh history command !em which ran the previously entered emacs command. The window status would show 'root:emacs' during the execution of the command, and revert to simply 'root:' at its completion.

```
bind o title
bind E title ""
bind u title (unknown)
```

The first binding doesn't have any arguments, so it would prompt you for a title when you type *C-a o*. The second binding would clear an auto-titles current setting (C-a E). The third binding would set the current window's title to '(unknown)' (C-a u).

10.2 Console

`console [`*`state`*`]`   [Command]
> (none)
> Grabs or un-grabs the machines console output to a window. When the argument
> is omitted the current state is displayed. *Note*: Only the owner of '`/dev/console`'
> can grab the console output. This command is only available if the host supports the
> ioctl `TIOCCONS`.

10.3 Kill

`kill`   [Command]
> (*C-a k*, *C-a C-k*)
> Kill the current window.
> If there is an **exec** command running (see Section 13.1 [Exec], page 61) then it is
> killed. Otherwise the process (e.g. shell) running in the window receives a `HANGUP`
> condition, the window structure is removed and screen (your display) switches to
> another window. When the last window is destroyed, **screen** exits. After a kill
> screen switches to the previously displayed window.
> *Caution*: **emacs** users may find themselves killing their **emacs** session when trying to
> delete the current line. For this reason, it is probably wise to use a different command
> character (see Section 14.3 [Command Character], page 64) or rebind `kill` to another
> key sequence, such as *C-a K* (see Chapter 14 [Key Binding], page 63).

10.4 Login

`deflogin` *state*   [Command]
> (none)
> Same as the **login** command except that the default setting for new windows
> is changed. This defaults to 'on' unless otherwise specified at compile time (see
> Chapter 26 [Installation], page 101). Both commands are only present when **screen**
> has been compiled with utmp support.

`login [`*`state`*`]`   [Command]
> (*C-a L*)
> Adds or removes the entry in '`/etc/utmp`' for the current window. This controls
> whether or not the window is *logged in*. In addition to this toggle, it is convenient
> to have "log in" and "log out" keys. For instance, **bind I login on** and **bind O
> login off** will map these keys to be *C-a I* and *C-a O* (see Chapter 14 [Key Binding],
> page 63).

10.5 Mode

`defmode` *mode*   [Command]
> (none)
> The mode of each newly allocated pseudo-tty is set to *mode*. *mode* is an octal number
> as used by chmod(1). Defaults to 0622 for windows which are logged in, 0600 for

others (e.g. when **-ln** was specified for creation, see Section 6.2 [Screen Command], page 25).

10.6 Monitoring

activity *message*   [Command]

(none)

When any activity occurs in a background window that is being monitored, **screen** displays a notification in the message line. The notification message can be redefined by means of the **activity** command. Each occurrence of '%' in *message* is replaced by the number of the window in which activity has occurred, and each occurrence of '^G' is replaced by the definition for bell in your termcap (usually an audible bell). The default message is

> 'Activity in window %n'

Note that monitoring is off for all windows by default, but can be altered by use of the **monitor** command (*C-a M*).

defmonitor *state*   [Command]

(none)

Same as the **monitor** command except that the default setting for new windows is changed. Initial setting is 'off'.

monitor [*state*]   [Command]

(*C-a M*)

Toggles monitoring of the current window. When monitoring is turned on and the affected window is switched into the background, the activity notification message will be displayed in the status line at the first sign of output, and the window will also be marked with an '@' in the window-status display (see Section 10.7 [Windows], page 42). Monitoring defaults to 'off' for all windows.

10.7 Windows

windows   [Command]

(*C-a w, C-a C-w*)

Uses the message line to display a list of all the windows. Each window is listed by number with the name of the program running in the window (or its title).

The current window is marked with a '*'; the previous window is marked with a '-'; all the windows that are logged in are marked with a '$' (see Section 10.4 [Login], page 41); a background window that has received a bell is marked with a '!'; a background window that is being monitored and has had activity occur is marked with an '@' (see Section 10.6 [Monitor], page 42); a window which has output logging turned on is marked with '(L)'; windows occupied by other users are marked with '&' or '&&' if the window is shared by other users; windows in the zombie state are marked with 'Z'.

If this list is too long to fit on the terminal's status line only the portion around the current window is displayed.

10.8 Hardstatus

`Screen` maintains a hardstatus line for every window. If a window gets selected, the display's hardstatus will be updated to match the window's hardstatus line. The hardstatus line can be changed with the ANSI Application Program Command (APC): '`ESC_<string>ESC\`'. As a convenience for xterm users the sequence '`ESC]0..2;<string>^G`' is also accepted.

defhstatus [*status*] [Command]
>   (none)
> The hardstatus line that all new windows will get is set to *status*. This command is useful to make the hardstatus of every window display the window number or title or the like. *status* may contain the same directives as in the window messages, but the directive escape character is '`^E`' (octal 005) instead of '`%`'. This was done to make a misinterpretation of program generated hardstatus lines impossible. If the parameter *status* is omitted, the current default string is displayed. Per default the hardstatus line of new windows is empty.

hstatus *status* [Command]
>   (none)
> Changes the current window's hardstatus line to *status*.

11 Virtual Terminal

Each window in a `screen` session emulates a VT100 terminal, with some extra functions
added. The VT100 emulator is hard-coded, no other terminal types can be emulated. The
commands described here modify the terminal emulation.

11.1 Control Sequences

The following is a list of control sequences recognized by `screen`. '(V)' and '(A)' indicate
VT100-specific and ANSI- or ISO-specific functions, respectively.

```
ESC E                         Next Line
ESC D                         Index
ESC M                         Reverse Index
ESC H                         Horizontal Tab Set
ESC Z                         Send VT100 Identification String
ESC 7              (V)        Save Cursor and Attributes
ESC 8              (V)        Restore Cursor and Attributes
ESC [s             (A)        Save Cursor and Attributes
ESC [u             (A)        Restore Cursor and Attributes
ESC c                         Reset to Initial State
ESC g                         Visual Bell
ESC Pn p                      Cursor Visibility (97801)
     Pn = 6                   Invisible
          7                   Visible
ESC =              (V)        Application Keypad Mode
ESC >              (V)        Numeric Keypad Mode
ESC # 8            (V)        Fill Screen with E's
ESC \              (A)        String Terminator
ESC ^              (A)        Privacy Message String (Message Line)
ESC !                         Global Message String (Message Line)
ESC k                         Title Definition String
ESC P              (A)        Device Control String
                              Outputs a string directly to the host
                              terminal without interpretation.

ESC _              (A)        Application Program Command (Hardstatus)
ESC ] 0 ; string ^G  (A)      Operating System Command (Hardstatus, xterm
                              title hack)
ESC ] 83 ; cmd ^G  (A)        Execute screen command. This only works if
                              multi-user support is compiled into screen.
                              The pseudo-user ":window:" is used to check
                              the access control list. Use "addacl :window:
                              -rwx #?" to create a user with no rights and
                              allow only the needed commands.
Control-N          (A)        Lock Shift G1 (SO)
Control-O          (A)        Lock Shift G0 (SI)
ESC n              (A)        Lock Shift G2
ESC o              (A)        Lock Shift G3
```

```
ESC N                       (A)     Single Shift G2
ESC O                       (A)     Single Shift G3
ESC ( Pcs                   (A)     Designate character set as G0
ESC ) Pcs                   (A)     Designate character set as G1
ESC * Pcs                   (A)     Designate character set as G2
ESC + Pcs                   (A)     Designate character set as G3
ESC [ Pn ; Pn H                     Direct Cursor Addressing
ESC [ Pn ; Pn f                     same as above
ESC [ Pn J                          Erase in Display
       Pn = None or 0               From Cursor to End of Screen
             1                      From Beginning of Screen to Cursor
             2                      Entire Screen
ESC [ Pn K                          Erase in Line
       Pn = None or 0               From Cursor to End of Line
             1                      From Beginning of Line to Cursor
             2                      Entire Line
ESC [ Pn X                          Erase character
ESC [ Pn A                          Cursor Up
ESC [ Pn B                          Cursor Down
ESC [ Pn C                          Cursor Right
ESC [ Pn D                          Cursor Left
ESC [ Pn E                          Cursor next line
ESC [ Pn F                          Cursor previous line
ESC [ Pn G                          Cursor horizontal position
ESC [ Pn `                          same as above
ESC [ Pn d                          Cursor vertical position
ESC [ Ps ;...; Ps m                 Select Graphic Rendition
       Ps = None or 0               Default Rendition
             1                      Bold
             2          (A)         Faint
             3          (A)         Standout Mode (ANSI: Italicized)
             4                      Underlined
             5                      Blinking
             7                      Negative Image
            22          (A)         Normal Intensity
            23          (A)         Standout Mode off (ANSI: Italicized off)
            24          (A)         Not Underlined
            25          (A)         Not Blinking
            27          (A)         Positive Image
            30          (A)         Foreground Black
            31          (A)         Foreground Red
            32          (A)         Foreground Green
            33          (A)         Foreground Yellow
            34          (A)         Foreground Blue
            35          (A)         Foreground Magenta
            36          (A)         Foreground Cyan
            37          (A)         Foreground White
```

```
                    39              (A)     Foreground Default
                    40              (A)     Background Black
                    ...                     ...
                    49              (A)     Background Default
        ESC [ Pn g                          Tab Clear
            Pn = None or 0                  Clear Tab at Current Position
                     3                      Clear All Tabs
        ESC [ Pn ; Pn r         (V)         Set Scrolling Region
        ESC [ Pn I              (A)         Horizontal Tab
        ESC [ Pn Z              (A)         Backward Tab
        ESC [ Pn L              (A)         Insert Line
        ESC [ Pn M              (A)         Delete Line
        ESC [ Pn @              (A)         Insert Character
        ESC [ Pn P              (A)         Delete Character
        ESC [ Pn S                          Scroll Scrolling Region Up
        ESC [ Pn T                          Scroll Scrolling Region Down
        ESC [ Pn ^                          same as above
        ESC [ Ps ;...; Ps h                 Set Mode
        ESC [ Ps ;...; Ps l                 Reset Mode
            Ps = 4             (A)          Insert Mode
                 20            (A)          'Automatic Linefeed' Mode.
                 34                         Normal Cursor Visibility
                 ?1            (V)          Application Cursor Keys
                 ?3            (V)          Change Terminal Width to 132 columns
                 ?5            (V)          Reverse Video
                 ?6            (V)          'Origin' Mode
                 ?7            (V)          'Wrap' Mode
                 ?9                         X10 mouse tracking
                 ?25           (V)          Visible Cursor
                 ?47                        Alternate Screen (old xterm code)
                 ?1000         (V)          VT200 mouse tracking
                 ?1047                      Alternate Screen (new xterm code)
                 ?1049                      Alternate Screen (new xterm code)
        ESC [ 5 i              (A)          Start relay to printer (ANSI Media Copy)
        ESC [ 4 i              (A)          Stop relay to printer (ANSI Media Copy)
        ESC [ 8 ; Ph ; Pw t                 Resize the window to 'Ph' lines and
                                            'Pw' columns (SunView special)
        ESC [ c                             Send VT100 Identification String
        ESC [ x                (V)          Send Terminal Parameter Report
        ESC [ > c                           Send Secondary Device Attributes String
        ESC [ 6 n                           Send Cursor Position Report
```

11.2 Input Translation

In order to do a full VT100 emulation **screen** has to detect that a sequence of characters in the input stream was generated by a keypress on the user's keyboard and insert the VT100 style escape sequence. **Screen** has a very flexible way of doing this by making it possible to map arbitrary commands on arbitrary sequences of characters. For standard VT100 emulation the command will always insert a string in the input buffer of the window (see also command **stuff**, see Section 12.2 [Paste], page 57). Because the sequences generated by a keypress can change after a reattach from a different terminal type, it is possible to bind commands to the termcap name of the keys. **Screen** will insert the correct binding after each reattach. See Section 14.5 [Bindkey], page 64 for further details on the syntax and examples.

Here is the table of the default key bindings. (A) means that the command is executed if the keyboard is switched into application mode.

```
Key name            Termcap name    Command
-------------------------------------------------------------
Cursor up           ku              stuff \033[A
                                    stuff \033OA      (A)
Cursor down         kd              stuff \033[B
                                    stuff \033OB      (A)
Cursor right        kr              stuff \033[C
                                    stuff \033OC      (A)
Cursor left         kl              stuff \033[D
                                    stuff \033OD      (A)
Function key 0      k0              stuff \033[10~
Function key 1      k1              stuff \033OP
Function key 2      k2              stuff \033OQ
Function key 3      k3              stuff \033OR
Function key 4      k4              stuff \033OS
Function key 5      k5              stuff \033[15~
Function key 6      k6              stuff \033[17~
Function key 7      k7              stuff \033[18~
Function key 8      k8              stuff \033[19~
Function key 9      k9              stuff \033[20~
Function key 10     k;              stuff \033[21~
Function key 11     F1              stuff \033[23~
Function key 12     F2              stuff \033[24~
Home                kh              stuff \033[1~
End                 kH              stuff \033[4~
Insert              kI              stuff \033[2~
Delete              kD              stuff \033[3~
Page up             kP              stuff \033[5~
Page down           kN              stuff \033[6~
Keypad 0            f0              stuff 0
                                    stuff \033Op      (A)
Keypad 1            f1              stuff 1
                                    stuff \033Oq      (A)
Keypad 2            f2              stuff 2
                                    stuff \033Or      (A)
```

Keypad 3	f3	stuff 3	
		stuff \0330s	(A)
Keypad 4	f4	stuff 4	
		stuff \0330t	(A)
Keypad 5	f5	stuff 5	
		stuff \0330u	(A)
Keypad 6	f6	stuff 6	
		stuff \0330v	(A)
Keypad 7	f7	stuff 7	
		stuff \0330w	(A)
Keypad 8	f8	stuff 8	
		stuff \0330x	(A)
Keypad 9	f9	stuff 9	
		stuff \0330y	(A)
Keypad +	f+	stuff +	
		stuff \0330k	(A)
Keypad −	f−	stuff −	
		stuff \0330m	(A)
Keypad *	f*	stuff *	
		stuff \0330j	(A)
Keypad /	f/	stuff /	
		stuff \0330o	(A)
Keypad =	fq	stuff =	
		stuff \0330X	(A)
Keypad .	f.	stuff .	
		stuff \0330n	(A)
Keypad ,	f,	stuff ,	
		stuff \0330l	(A)
Keypad enter	fe	stuff \015	
		stuff \0330M	(A)

11.3 Digraph

digraph [*preset*]   [Command]
  (none)
  This command prompts the user for a digraph sequence. The next two characters
  typed are looked up in a builtin table and the resulting character is inserted in the
  input stream. For example, if the user enters 'a"', an a-umlaut will be inserted. If
  the first character entered is a 0 (zero), **screen** will treat the following characters (up
  to three) as an octal number instead. The optional argument *preset* is treated as user
  input, thus one can create an "umlaut" key. For example the command 'bindkey ^K
  digraph '"'' enables the user to generate an a-umlaut by typing 'CTRL-K a'.

11.4 Bell

`bell_msg` [*message*]   [Command]
>   (none)
>   When a bell character is sent to a background window, **screen** displays a notification
>   in the message line. The notification message can be re-defined by this command.
>   Each occurrence of '%' in *message* is replaced by the number of the window to which
>   a bell has been sent, and each occurrence of '^G' is replaced by the definition for bell
>   in your termcap (usually an audible bell). The default message is
>
>>   'Bell in window %n'
>
>   An empty message can be supplied to the `bell_msg` command to suppress output of
>   a message line (`bell_msg ""`). Without parameter, the current message is shown.

`vbell` [*state*]   [Command]
>   (`C-a C-g`)
>   Sets or toggles the visual bell setting for the current window. If **vbell** is switched
>   to 'on', but your terminal does not support a visual bell, the visual bell message is
>   displayed in the status line when the bell character is received. Visual bell support
>   of a terminal is defined by the termcap variable **vb**. See Section "Visual Bell" in
>   *The Termcap Manual*, for more information on visual bells. The equivalent terminfo
>   capability is **flash**.
>
>   Per default, **vbell** is 'off', thus the audible bell is used.

`vbell_msg` [*message*]   [Command]
>   (none)
>   Sets the visual bell message. *Message* is printed to the status line if the window
>   receives a bell character (^G), **vbell** is set to 'on' and the terminal does not support
>   a visual bell. The default message is 'Wuff, Wuff!!'. Without parameter, the current
>   message is shown.

`vbellwait` *sec*   [Command]
>   (none)
>   Define a delay in seconds after each display of **screen**'s visual bell message. The
>   default is 1 second.

11.5 Clear

`clear`   [Command]
>   (`C-a C`)
>   Clears the screen and saves its contents to the scrollback buffer.

11.6 Info

`info`   [Command]
>   (`C-a i, C-a C-i`)
>   Uses the message line to display some information about the current window: the
>   cursor position in the form '(`column,row`)' starting with '(1,1)', the terminal width

and height plus the size of the scrollback buffer in lines, like in '(80,24)+50', the current state of window XON/XOFF flow control is shown like this (see Chapter 15 [Flow Control], page 67):

```
+flow       automatic flow control, currently on.
-flow       automatic flow control, currently off.
+(+)flow    flow control enabled. Agrees with automatic control.
-(+)flow    flow control disabled. Disagrees with automatic control.
+(-)flow    flow control enabled. Disagrees with automatic control.
-(-)flow    flow control disabled. Agrees with automatic control.
```

The current line wrap setting ('+wrap' indicates enabled, '-wrap' not) is also shown. The flags 'ins', 'org', 'app', 'log', 'mon' and 'nored' are displayed when the window is in insert mode, origin mode, application-keypad mode, has output logging, activity monitoring or partial redraw enabled.

The currently active character set ('G0', 'G1', 'G2', or 'G3'), and in square brackets the terminal character sets that are currently designated as 'G0' through 'G3'. If the window is in UTF-8 mode, the string 'UTF-8' is shown instead. Additional modes depending on the type of the window are displayed at the end of the status line (see Section 6.6 [Window Types], page 26).

If the state machine of the terminal emulator is in a non-default state, the info line is started with a string identifying the current state.

For system information use **time**.

dinfo   [Command]

(none)

Show what screen thinks about your terminal. Useful if you want to know why features like color or the alternate charset don't work.

11.7 Redisplay

allpartial *state*   [Command]

(none)

If set to on, only the current cursor line is refreshed on window change. This affects all windows and is useful for slow terminal lines. The previous setting of full/partial refresh for each window is restored with **allpartial off**. This is a global flag that immediately takes effect on all windows overriding the **partial** settings. It does not change the default redraw behavior of newly created windows.

altscreen *state*   [Command]

(none)

If set to on, "alternate screen" support is enabled in virtual terminals, just like in xterm. Initial setting is 'off'.

partial *state*   [Command]

(none)

Defines whether the display should be refreshed (as with **redisplay**) after switching to the current window. This command only affects the current window. To immediately affect all windows use the **allpartial** command. Default is 'off', of course. This default is fixed, as there is currently no **defpartial** command.

redisplay   [Command]
>   (*C-a l, C-a C-l*)
>   Redisplay the current window. Needed to get a full redisplay in partial redraw mode.

11.8 Wrap

wrap *state*   [Command]
>   (*C-a r, C-a C-r*)
>   Sets the line-wrap setting for the current window. When line-wrap is on, the second
>   consecutive printable character output at the last column of a line will wrap to the
>   start of the following line. As an added feature, backspace (^H) will also wrap through
>   the left margin to the previous line. Default is 'on'.

defwrap *state*   [Command]
>   (none)
>   Same as the **wrap** command except that the default setting for new windows is
>   changed. Initially line-wrap is on and can be toggled with the **wrap** command (*C-a
>   r*) or by means of "C-a : wrap on|off".

11.9 Reset

reset   [Command]
>   (*C-a Z*)
>   Reset the virtual terminal to its "power-on" values. Useful when strange settings (like
>   scroll regions or graphics character set) are left over from an application.

11.10 Window Size

width [-w|-d] [*cols* [*lines*]]   [Command]
>   (*C-a W*)
>   Toggle the window width between 80 and 132 columns, or set it to *cols* columns if an
>   argument is specified. This requires a capable terminal and the termcap entries 'Z0'
>   and 'Z1'. See the **termcap** command (see Chapter 16 [Termcap], page 69), for more
>   information. You can also specify a height if you want to change both values. The -w
>   option tells screen to leave the display size unchanged and just set the window size,
>   -d vice versa.

height [-w|-d] [*lines* [*cols*]]   [Command]
>   (none)
>   Set the display height to a specified number of lines. When no argument is given it
>   toggles between 24 and 42 lines display.

11.11 Character Processing

c1 [*state*]   [Command]
>   (none)
>   Change c1 code processing. 'c1 on' tells screen to treat the input characters between

128 and 159 as control functions. Such an 8-bit code is normally the same as ESC
followed by the corresponding 7-bit code. The default setting is to process c1 codes
and can be changed with the 'defc1' command. Users with fonts that have usable
characters in the c1 positions may want to turn this off.

gr [*state*]   [Command]
(none)
Turn GR charset switching on/off. Whenever screen sees an input char with an 8th
bit set, it will use the charset stored in the GR slot and print the character with
the 8th bit stripped. The default (see also 'defgr') is not to process GR switching
because otherwise the ISO88591 charset would not work.

bce [*state*]   [Command]
(none)
Change background-color-erase setting. If 'bce' is set to on, all characters cleared
by an erase/insert/scroll/clear operation will be displayed in the current background
color. Otherwise the default background color is used.

encoding *enc* [*denc*]   [Command]
(none)
Tell screen how to interpret the input/output. The first argument sets the encoding
of the current window. Each window can emulate a different encoding. The optional
second parameter overwrites the encoding of the connected terminal. It should never
be needed as screen uses the locale setting to detect the encoding. There is also a
way to select a terminal encoding depending on the terminal type by using the 'KJ'
termcap entry. See Section 16.5 [Special Capabilities], page 72.

Supported encodings are eucJP, SJIS, eucKR, eucCN, Big5, GBK, KOI8-R, CP1251,
UTF-8, ISO8859-2, ISO8859-3, ISO8859-4, ISO8859-5, ISO8859-6, ISO8859-7,
ISO8859-8, ISO8859-9, ISO8859-10, ISO8859-15, jis.

See also 'defencoding', which changes the default setting of a new window.

charset *set*   [Command]
(none)
Change the current character set slot designation and charset mapping. The first four
character of *set* are treated as charset designators while the fifth and sixth character
must be in range '0' to '3' and set the GL/GR charset mapping. On every position
a '.' may be used to indicate that the corresponding charset/mapping should not
be changed (*set* is padded to six characters internally by appending '.' chars). New
windows have 'BBBB02' as default charset, unless a 'encoding' command is active.

The current setting can be viewed with the Section 11.6 [Info], page 50 command.

utf8 [*state* [*dstate*]]   [Command]
(none)
Change the encoding used in the current window. If utf8 is enabled, the strings sent
to the window will be UTF-8 encoded and vice versa. Omitting the parameter toggles
the setting. If a second parameter is given, the display's encoding is also changed (this
should rather be done with screen's '-U' option). See also 'defutf8', which changes
the default setting of a new window.

defc1 *state*   [Command]

> (none)
> Same as the 'c1' command except that the default setting for new windows is changed.
> Initial setting is 'on'.

defgr *state*   [Command]

> (none)
> Same as the 'gr' command except that the default setting for new windows is changed.
> Initial setting is 'off'.

defbce *state*   [Command]

> (none)
> Same as the 'bce' command except that the default setting for new windows is
> changed. Initial setting is 'off'.

defencoding *enc*   [Command]

> (none)
> Same as the 'encoding' command except that the default setting for new windows is
> changed. Initial setting is the encoding taken from the terminal.

defcharset [*set*]   [Command]

> Like the 'charset' command except that the default setting for new windows is
> changed. Shows current default if called without argument.

defutf8 *state*   [Command]

> (none)
> Same as the 'utf8' command except that the default setting for new windows is
> changed. Initial setting is **on** if screen was started with '-U', otherwise **off**.

12 Copy and Paste

For those confined to a hardware terminal, these commands provide a cut and paste facility more powerful than those provided by most windowing systems.

12.1 Copying

copy   [Command]

> (*C-a [*, *C-a C-[*, *C-a ESC*)
> Enter copy/scrollback mode. This allows you to copy text from the current window and its history into the paste buffer. In this mode a vi-like full screen editor is active, with controls as outlined below.

12.1.1 CR/LF

crlf [*state*]   [Command]

> (none)
> This affects the copying of text regions with the *C-a [* command. If it is set to 'on', lines will be separated by the two character sequence 'CR'/'LF'. Otherwise only 'LF' is used. **crlf** is off by default. When no parameter is given, the state is toggled.

12.1.2 Scrollback

defscrollback *num*   [Command]

> (none)
> Same as the **scrollback** command except that the default setting for new windows is changed. Defaults to 100.

scrollback *num*   [Command]

> (none)
> Set the size of the scrollback buffer for the current window to *num* lines. The default scrollback is 100 lines. Use *C-a i* to view the current setting.

compacthist [*state*]   [Command]

> (none)
> This tells screen whether to suppress trailing blank lines when scrolling up text into the history buffer. Turn compacting 'on' to hold more useful lines in your scrollback buffer.

12.1.3 markkeys

markkeys *string*   [Command]

> (none)
> This is a method of changing the keymap used for copy/history mode. The string is made up of *oldchar=newchar* pairs which are separated by ':'. Example: The command **markkeys h=^B:l=^F:$=^E** would set some keys to be more familiar to **emacs** users. If your terminal sends characters, that cause you to abort copy mode, then this command may help by binding these characters to do nothing. The no-op character is '@' and is used like this: **markkeys @=L=H** if you do not want to use the

'H' or 'L' commands any longer. As shown in this example, multiple keys can be assigned to one function in a single statement.

12.1.4 Movement Keys

h, *j*, *k*, *l* move the cursor line by line or column by column.

0, ^ and *$* move to the leftmost column or to the first or last non-whitespace character on the line.

H, *M* and *L* move the cursor to the leftmost column of the top, center or bottom line of the window.

+ and *−* move the cursor to the leftmost column of the next or previous line.

G moves to the specified absolute line (default: end of buffer).

| moves to the specified absolute column.

w, *b*, *e* move the cursor word by word.

B, *E* move the cursor WORD by WORD (as in vi).

C-u and *C-d* scroll the display up/down by the specified amount of lines while preserving the cursor position. (Default: half screenful).

C-b and *C-f* move the cursor up/down a full screen.

g moves to the beginning of the buffer.

% jumps to the specified percentage of the buffer.

Note that Emacs-style movement keys can be specified by a .screenrc command. (`markkeys "h=^B:l=^F:$=^E"`) There is no simple method for a full emacs-style keymap, however, as this involves multi-character codes.

12.1.5 Marking

The copy range is specified by setting two marks. The text between these marks will be highlighted. Press *space* to set the first or second mark respectively.

Y and *y* can be used to mark one whole line or to mark from start of line.

W marks exactly one word.

12.1.6 Repeat Count

Any command in copy mode can be prefixed with a number (by pressing digits *0...9*) which is taken as a repeat count. Example: *C-a C-[H 10 j 5 Y* will copy lines 11 to 15 into the paste buffer.

12.1.7 Searching

/ vi-like search forward.

? vi-like search backward.

C-a s emacs style incremental search forward.

C-r emacs style reverse i-search.

ignorecase [*state*]   [Command]
        (none)
        Tell screen to ignore the case of characters in searches. Default is **off**.

12.1.8 Specials

There are, however, some keys that act differently here from in vi. Vi does not allow to yank rectangular blocks of text, but screen does. Press

c or C to set the left or right margin respectively. If no repeat count is given, both default to the current cursor position.

Example: Try this on a rather full text screen: C-a [M 20 l SPACE c 10 l 5 j C SPACE.

This moves one to the middle line of the screen, moves in 20 columns left, marks the beginning of the paste buffer, sets the left column, moves 5 columns down, sets the right column, and then marks the end of the paste buffer. Now try:

C-a [M 20 l SPACE 10 l 5 j SPACE

and notice the difference in the amount of text copied.

J joins lines. It toggles between 4 modes: lines separated by a newline character (012), lines glued seamless, lines separated by a single space or comma separated lines. Note that you can prepend the newline character with a carriage return character, by issuing a set crlf on.

v is for all the vi users who use :set numbers - it toggles the left margin between column 9 and 1.

a before the final space key turns on append mode. Thus the contents of the paste buffer will not be overwritten, but appended to.

A turns on append mode and sets a (second) mark.

> sets the (second) mark and writes the contents of the paste buffer to the screen-exchange file ('/tmp/screen-exchange' per default) once copy-mode is finished. See Section 12.4 [Screen Exchange], page 59.

This example demonstrates how to dump the whole scrollback buffer to that file:

C-a [g SPACE G $ >.

C-g gives information about the current line and column.

x exchanges the first mark and the current cursor position. You can use this to adjust an already placed mark.

@ does nothing. Absolutely nothing. Does not even exit copy mode.

All keys not described here exit copy mode.

12.2 Paste

paste [registers [destination]]   [Command]
    (C-a], C-a C-])

        Write the (concatenated) contents of the specified registers to the stdin stream of the current window. The register '.' is treated as the paste buffer. If no parameter is specified the user is prompted to enter a single register. The paste buffer can be filled with the copy, history and readbuf commands. Other registers can be filled with the register, readreg and paste commands. If paste is called with a second argument, the contents of the specified registers is pasted into the named destination register rather than the window. If '.' is used as the second argument, the display's paste buffer is the destination. Note, that paste uses a wide variety of resources: Usually both, a current window and a current display are required. But whenever a second argument is specified no current window is needed. When the source specification only contains registers (not the paste buffer) then there need not be a current display (terminal attached), as the registers are a global resource. The paste buffer exists once for every user.

stuff *string*   [Command]

(none)

Stuff the string *string* in the input buffer of the current window. This is like the **paste** command, but with much less overhead. You cannot paste large buffers with the **stuff** command. It is most useful for key bindings. See Section 14.5 [Bindkey], page 64.

pastefont [*state*]   [Command]

Tell screen to include font information in the paste buffer. The default is not to do so. This command is especially useful for multi character fonts like kanji.

slowpaste *msec*   [Command]
defslowpaste *msec*   [Command]

(none)

Define the speed text is inserted in the current window by the **paste** command. If the slowpaste value is nonzero text is written character by character. **screen** will pause for *msec* milliseconds after each write to allow the application to process the input. only use **slowpaste** if your underlying system exposes flow control problems while pasting large amounts of text. **defslowpaste** specifies the default for new windows.

readreg [*-e encoding*] [*register* [*filename*]]   [Command]

(none)

Does one of two things, dependent on number of arguments: with zero or one arguments it it duplicates the paste buffer contents into the register specified or entered at the prompt. With two arguments it reads the contents of the named file into the register, just as **readbuf** reads the screen-exchange file into the paste buffer. You can tell screen the encoding of the file via the **-e** option. The following example will paste the system's password file into the screen window (using register p, where a copy remains):

```
C-a : readreg p /etc/passwd
C-a : paste p
```

12.3 Registers

copy_reg [*key*]   [Command]

(none)

Removed. Use **readreg** instead.

ins_reg [*key*]   [Command]

(none)

Removed. Use **paste** instead.

process [*key*]   [Command]

(none)

Stuff the contents of the specified register into the **screen** input queue. If no argument is given you are prompted for a register name. The text is parsed as if it had been typed in from the user's keyboard. This command can be used to bind multiple actions to a single key.

register [*-e encoding*] *key string*   [Command]
>   (none)
>   Save the specified *string* to the register *key*. The encoding of the string can be specified via the **-e** option.

12.4 Screen Exchange

bufferfile [*exchange-file*]   [Command]
>   (none)
>   Change the filename used for reading and writing with the paste buffer. If the *exchange-file* parameter is omitted, **screen** reverts to the default of '/tmp/screen-exchange'. The following example will paste the system's password file into the screen window (using the paste buffer, where a copy remains):
>
> ```
> C-a : bufferfile /etc/passwd
> C-a < C-a ]
> C-a : bufferfile
> ```

readbuf [*-e encoding*] [*filename*]   [Command]
>   (*C-a <*)
>   Reads the contents of the specified file into the paste buffer. You can tell screen the encoding of the file via the **-e** option. If no file is specified, the screen-exchange filename is used.

removebuf   [Command]
>   (*C-a =*)
>   Unlinks the screen-exchange file.

writebuf [*-e encoding*] [*filename*]   [Command]
>   (*C-a >*)
>   Writes the contents of the paste buffer to the specified file, or the public accessible screen-exchange file if no filename is given. This is thought of as a primitive means of communication between **screen** users on the same host. If an encoding is specified the paste buffer is recoded on the fly to match the encoding. See also *C-a ESC* (see Section 12.1 [Copy], page 55).

12.5 History

history   [Command]
>   (*C-a {*)
>   Usually users work with a shell that allows easy access to previous commands. For example, **csh** has the command !! to repeat the last command executed. **screen** provides a primitive way of recalling "the command that started ...": You just type the first letter of that command, then hit *C-a {* and **screen** tries to find a previous line that matches with the prompt character to the left of the cursor. This line is

pasted into this window's input queue. Thus you have a crude command history (made up by the visible window and its scrollback buffer).

13 Subprocess Execution

Control Input or Output of a window by another filter process. Use with care!

13.1 Exec

exec [[*fdpat*] newcommand [args ...]]   [Command]
        (none)

        Run a unix subprocess (specified by an executable path *newcommand* and its op-
tional arguments) in the current window. The flow of data between newcommands
stdin/stdout/stderr, the process originally started (let us call it "application-process")
and screen itself (window) is controlled by the file descriptor pattern *fdpat*. This pattern is basically a three character sequence representing stdin, stdout and stderr of
newcommand. A dot (.) connects the file descriptor to screen. An exclamation mark
(!) causes the file descriptor to be connected to the application-process. A colon (:)
combines both.

        User input will go to newcommand unless newcommand receives the application-
process' output (*fdpat*s first character is '!' or ':') or a pipe symbol ('|') is added to
the end of *fdpat*.

        Invoking exec without arguments shows name and arguments of the currently run-
ning subprocess in this window. Only one subprocess can be running per window.

        When a subprocess is running the kill command will affect it instead of the windows
process. Only one subprocess a time can be running in each window.

        Refer to the postscript file 'doc/fdpat.ps' for a confusing illustration of all 21 pos-
sible combinations. Each drawing shows the digits 2, 1, 0 representing the three
file descriptors of newcommand. The box marked 'W' is usual pty that has the
application-process on its slave side. The box marked 'P' is the secondary pty that
now has screen at its master side.

13.2 Using Exec

Abbreviations:

- Whitespace between the word 'exec' and *fdpat* and the command name can be omitted.

- Trailing dots and a *fdpat* consisting only of dots can be omitted.

- A simple '|' is synonymous for the '!..|' pattern.

- The word 'exec' can be omitted when the '|' abbreviation is used.

- The word 'exec' can always be replaced by leading '!'.

Examples:

```
!/bin/sh
exec /bin/sh
exec ... /bin/sh
```

        All of the above are equivalent. Creates another shell in the same window,
while the original shell is still running. Output of both shells is displayed and
user input is sent to the new '/bin/sh'.

```
!!stty 19200
exec!stty 19200
exec !.. stty 19200
```
> All of the above are equivalent. Set the speed of the window's tty. If your stty command operates on stdout, then add another '!'. This is a useful command, when a screen window is directly connected to a serial line that needs to be configured.

```
|less
exec !..| less
```
> Both are equivalent. This adds a pager to the window output. The special character '|' is needed to give the user control over the pager although it gets its input from the window's process. This works, because '**less**' listens on stderr (a behavior that **screen** would not expect without the '|') when its stdin is not a tty. **Less** versions newer than 177 fail miserably here; good old **pg** still works.

```
!:sed -n s/.*Error.*/\007/p
```
> Sends window output to both, the user and the sed command. The sed inserts an additional bell character (oct. 007) to the window output seen by screen. This will cause 'Bell in window x' messages, whenever the string '**Error**' appears in the window.

14 Key Binding

You may disagree with some of the default bindings (I know I do). The `bind` command allows you to redefine them to suit your preferences.

14.1 The bind command

`bind` [-c class] key [command [args]]   [Command]
  (none)

> Bind a command to a key. The *key* argument is either a single character, a two-character sequence of the form '^x' (meaning C-x), a backslash followed by an octal number (specifying the ASCII code of the character), or a backslash followed by a second character, such as '\^' or '\\'. The argument can also be quoted, if you like. If no further argument is given, any previously established binding for this key is removed. The *command* argument can be any command (see [Command Index], page 105).

> If a command class is specified via the -c option, the key is bound for the specified class. Use the `command` command to activate a class. Command classes can be used to create multiple command keys or multi-character bindings.

> By default, most suitable commands are bound to one or more keys (see Section 5.1 [Default Key Bindings], page 11; for instance, the command to create a new window is bound to C-c and c. The `bind` command can be used to redefine the key bindings and to define new bindings.

14.2 Examples of the bind command

Some examples:

```
bind ' ' windows
bind ^f screen telnet foobar
bind \033 screen -ln -t root -h 1000 9 su
```

would bind the space key to the command that displays a list of windows (so that the command usually invoked by C-a C-w would also be available as C-a space), bind C-f to the command "create a window with a TELNET connection to foobar", and bind ESC to the command that creates an non-login window with title 'root' in slot #9, with a superuser shell and a scrollback buffer of 1000 lines.

```
bind -c demo1 0 select 10
bind -c demo1 1 select 11
bind -c demo1 2 select 12
bindkey "^B" command -c demo1
```

makes C-b 0 select window 10, C-b 1 window 11, etc.

```
bind -c demo2 0 select 10
bind -c demo2 1 select 11
bind -c demo2 2 select 12
bind - command -c demo2
```

makes C-a - 0 select window 10, C-a - 1 window 11, etc.

14.3 Command Character

escape *xy*   [Command]
> (none)
>
> Set the command character to *x* and the character generating a literal command
> character (by triggering the meta command) to *y* (similar to the '-e' option). Each
> argument is either a single character, a two-character sequence of the form '^x' (mean-
> ing *C-x*), a backslash followed by an octal number (specifying the ASCII code of the
> character), or a backslash followed by a second character, such as '\^' or '\\'. The
> default is '^Aa', but '' is recommended by one of the authors.

defescape *xy*   [Command]
> (none)
>
> Set the default command characters. This is equivalent to the command escape
> except that it is useful for multiuser sessions only. In a multiuser session escape
> changes the command character of the calling user, where defescape changes the
> default command characters for users that will be added later.

meta   [Command]
> (*C-a* a)
>
> Send the command character (*C-a*) to the process in the current window. The
> keystroke for this command is the second parameter to the '-e' command line switch
> (see Chapter 3 [Invoking Screen], page 5), or the escape .screenrc directive.

command [-c *class*]   [Command]
> (none)
>
> This command has the same effect as typing the screen escape character (*C-a*). It is
> probably only useful for key bindings. If the '-c' option is given, select the specified
> command class. See Section 14.1 [Bind], page 63, See Section 14.5 [Bindkey], page 64.

14.4 Help

help   [Command]
> (*C-a* ?)
>
> Displays a help screen showing you all the key bindings. The first pages list all the
> internal commands followed by their bindings. Subsequent pages will display the
> custom commands, one command per key. Press space when you're done reading
> each page, or return to exit early. All other characters are ignored. If the '-c' option
> is given, display all bound commands for the specified command class. See Section 5.1
> [Default Key Bindings], page 11.

14.5 Bindkey

bindkey [*opts*] [*string* [*cmd args*]]   [Command]
> (none)
>
> This command manages screen's input translation tables. Every entry in one of the
> tables tells screen how to react if a certain sequence of characters is encountered.
> There are three tables: one that should contain actions programmed by the user, one

for the default actions used for terminal emulation and one for screen's copy mode to do cursor movement. See Section 11.2 [Input Translation], page 47 for a list of default key bindings.

If the '-d' option is given, bindkey modifies the default table, '-m' changes the copy mode table and with neither option the user table is selected. The argument 'string' is the sequence of characters to which an action is bound. This can either be a fixed string or a termcap keyboard capability name (selectable with the '-k' option).

Some keys on a VT100 terminal can send a different string if application mode is turned on (e.g. the cursor keys). Such keys have two entries in the translation table. You can select the application mode entry by specifying the '-a' option.

The '-t' option tells screen not to do inter-character timing. One cannot turn off the timing if a termcap capability is used.

'cmd' can be any of screen's commands with an arbitrary number of 'args'. If 'cmd' is omitted the key-binding is removed from the table.

14.6 Bindkey Examples

Here are some examples of keyboard bindings:

    bindkey -d

Show all of the default key bindings. The application mode entries are marked with [A].

    bindkey -k k1 select 1

Make the "F1" key switch to window one.

    bindkey -t foo stuff barfoo

Make 'foo' an abbreviation of the word 'barfoo'. Timeout is disabled so that users can type slowly.

    bindkey "\024" mapdefault

This key-binding makes 'C-t' an escape character for key-bindings. If you did the above 'stuff barfoo' binding, you can enter the word 'foo' by typing 'C-t foo'. If you want to insert a 'C-t' you have to press the key twice (i.e., escape the escape binding).

    bindkey -k F1 command

Make the F11 (not F1!) key an alternative screen escape (besides 'C-a').

14.7 Bindkey Control

mapdefault   [Command]
    (none)
    Tell screen that the next input character should only be looked up in the default bindkey table.

mapnotnext   [Command]
    (none)
    Like mapdefault, but don't even look in the default bindkey table.

`maptimeout` *timo*   [Command]
     (none)
     Set the inter-character timer for input sequence detection to a timeout of *timo* ms.
     The default timeout is 300ms. Maptimeout with no arguments shows the current
     setting.

15 Flow Control

screen can trap flow control characters or pass them to the program, as you see fit. This is useful when your terminal wants to use XON/XOFF flow control and you are running a program which wants to use ^S/^Q for other purposes (i.e. **emacs**).

15.1 About screen flow control settings

Each window has a flow-control setting that determines how screen deals with the XON and XOFF characters (and perhaps the interrupt character). When flow-control is turned off, screen ignores the XON and XOFF characters, which allows the user to send them to the current program by simply typing them (useful for the **emacs** editor, for instance). The trade-off is that it will take longer for output from a "normal" program to pause in response to an XOFF. With flow-control turned on, XON and XOFF characters are used to immediately pause the output of the current window. You can still send these characters to the current program, but you must use the appropriate two-character screen commands (typically *C-a q* (xon) and *C-a s* (xoff)). The xon/xoff commands are also useful for typing C-s and C-q past a terminal that intercepts these characters.

Each window has an initial flow-control value set with either the '-f' option or the **defflow** command. By default the windows are set to automatic flow-switching. It can then be toggled between the three states 'fixed on', 'fixed off' and 'automatic' interactively with the **flow** command bound to *C-a f*.

The automatic flow-switching mode deals with flow control using the TIOCPKT mode (like **rlogin** does). If the tty driver does not support TIOCPKT, screen tries to determine the right mode based on the current setting of the application keypad — when it is enabled, flow-control is turned off and visa versa. Of course, you can still manipulate flow-control manually when needed.

If you're running with flow-control enabled and find that pressing the interrupt key (usually C-c) does not interrupt the display until another 6-8 lines have scrolled by, try running screen with the '**interrupt**' option (add the '**interrupt**' flag to the **flow** command in your .screenrc, or use the '-i' command-line option). This causes the output that **screen** has accumulated from the interrupted program to be flushed. One disadvantage is that the virtual terminal's memory contains the non-flushed version of the output, which in rare cases can cause minor inaccuracies in the output. For example, if you switch screens and return, or update the screen with *C-a l* you would see the version of the output you would have gotten without '**interrupt**' being on. Also, you might need to turn off flow-control (or use auto-flow mode to turn it off automatically) when running a program that expects you to type the interrupt character as input, as the '**interrupt**' parameter only takes effect when flow-control is enabled. If your program's output is interrupted by mistake, a simple refresh of the screen with *C-a l* will restore it. Give each mode a try, and use whichever mode you find more comfortable.

15.2 Flow

defflow *fstate* [*interrupt*]   [Command]

    (none)

        Same as the **flow** command except that the default setting for new windows is changed. Initial setting is 'auto'. Specifying `flow auto interrupt` has the same effect as the command-line options '`-fa`' and '`-i`'. Note that if '`interrupt`' is enabled, all existing displays are changed immediately to forward interrupt signals.

`flow` [*fstate*]   [Command]
(*C*-a *f*, *C*-a *C*-*f*)
Sets the flow-control mode for this window to *fstate*, which can be 'on', 'off' or 'auto'. Without parameters it cycles the current window's flow-control setting. Default is set by 'defflow'.

15.3 XON and XOFF

`xon`   [Command]
(*C*-a *q*, *C*-a *C*-*q*)
Send a ^Q (ASCII XON) to the program in the current window. Redundant if flow control is set to 'off' or 'auto'.

`xoff`   [Command]
(*C*-a *s*, *C*-a *C*-*s*)
Send a ^S (ASCII XOFF) to the program in the current window.

16 Termcap

`screen` demands the most out of your terminal so that it can perform its VT100 emulation most efficiently. These functions provide means for tweaking the termcap entries for both your physical terminal and the one simulated by `screen`.

16.1 Choosing the termcap entry for a window

Usually `screen` tries to emulate as much of the VT100/ANSI standard as possible. But if your terminal lacks certain capabilities the emulation may not be complete. In these cases `screen` has to tell the applications that some of the features are missing. This is no problem on machines using termcap, because `screen` can use the `$TERMCAP` variable to customize the standard screen termcap.

But if you do a rlogin on another machine or your machine supports only terminfo this method fails. Because of this `screen` offers a way to deal with these cases. Here is how it works:

When `screen` tries to figure out a terminal name for itself, it first looks for an entry named `screen.term`, where *term* is the contents of your `$TERM` variable. If no such entry exists, `screen` tries 'screen' (or 'screen-w', if the terminal is wide (132 cols or more)). If even this entry cannot be found, 'vt100' is used as a substitute.

The idea is that if you have a terminal which doesn't support an important feature (e.g. delete char or clear to EOS) you can build a new termcap/terminfo entry for `screen` (named 'screen.*dumbterm*') in which this capability has been disabled. If this entry is installed on your machines you are able to do a rlogin and still keep the correct termcap/terminfo entry. The terminal name is put in the `$TERM` variable of all new windows. `screen` also sets the `$TERMCAP` variable reflecting the capabilities of the virtual terminal emulated. Furthermore, the variable `$WINDOW` is set to the window number of each window.

The actual set of capabilities supported by the virtual terminal depends on the capabilities supported by the physical terminal. If, for instance, the physical terminal does not support underscore mode, `screen` does not put the 'us' and 'ue' capabilities into the window's `$TERMCAP` variable, accordingly. However, a minimum number of capabilities must be supported by a terminal in order to run `screen`; namely scrolling, clear screen, and direct cursor addressing (in addition, `screen` does not run on hardcopy terminals or on terminals that over-strike).

Also, you can customize the `$TERMCAP` value used by `screen` by using the `termcap` command, or by defining the variable `$SCREENCAP` prior to startup. When the latter defined, its value will be copied verbatim into each window's `$TERMCAP` variable. This can either be the full terminal definition, or a filename where the terminal 'screen' (and/or 'screen-w') is defined.

Note that `screen` honors the `terminfo` command if the system uses the terminfo database rather than termcap. On such machines the `$TERMCAP` variable has no effect and you must use the `dumptermcap` command (see Section 16.2 [Dump Termcap], page 70) and the `tic` program to generate terminfo entries for `screen` windows.

When the boolean 'G0' capability is present in the termcap entry for the terminal on which `screen` has been called, the terminal emulation of `screen` supports multiple character sets. This allows an application to make use of, for instance, the VT100 graphics character set or national character sets. The following control functions from ISO 2022 are supported: 'lock shift G0' ('SI'), 'lock shift G1' ('SO'), 'lock shift G2', 'lock shift G3', 'single shift G2', and 'single shift G3'. When a virtual terminal is created or reset, the ASCII character set is designated as 'G0' through 'G3'. When the 'G0' capability is present, screen evaluates the capabilities 'S0', 'E0', and 'C0' if present. 'S0' is the sequence the terminal uses to enable and start the graphics character set rather than 'SI'. 'E0' is the corresponding replacement for 'SO'. 'C0' gives a character by character translation string that is used during semi-graphics mode. This string is built like the 'acsc' terminfo capability.

When the 'po' and 'pf' capabilities are present in the terminal's termcap entry, applications running in a screen window can send output to the printer port of the terminal. This allows a user to have an application in one window sending output to a printer connected to the terminal, while all other windows are still active (the printer port is enabled and disabled again for each chunk of output). As a side-effect, programs running in different windows can send output to the printer simultaneously. Data sent to the printer is not displayed in the window. The info command displays a line starting with 'PRIN' while the printer is active.

Some capabilities are only put into the $TERMCAP variable of the virtual terminal if they can be efficiently implemented by the physical terminal. For instance, 'dl' (delete line) is only put into the $TERMCAP variable if the terminal supports either delete line itself or scrolling regions. Note that this may provoke confusion, when the session is reattached on a different terminal, as the value of $TERMCAP cannot be modified by parent processes. You can force screen to include all capabilities in $TERMCAP with the '-a' command-line option (see Chapter 3 [Invoking Screen], page 5).

The "alternate screen" capability is not enabled by default. Set the altscreen '.screenrc' command to enable it.

16.2 Write out the window's termcap entry

dumptermcap   [Command]
    (C-a .)
    Write the termcap entry for the virtual terminal optimized for the currently active window to the file '.termcap' in the user's '$HOME/.screen' directory (or wherever screen stores its sockets. see Chapter 23 [Files], page 95). This termcap entry is identical to the value of the environment variable $TERMCAP that is set up by screen for each window. For terminfo based systems you will need to run a converter like captoinfo and then compile the entry with tic.

16.3 The termcap command

termcap *term terminal-tweaks* [*window-tweaks*]   [Command]
terminfo *term terminal-tweaks* [*window-tweaks*]   [Command]
termcapinfo *term terminal-tweaks* [*window-tweaks*]   [Command]
    (none)
    Use this command to modify your terminal's termcap entry without going through all the hassles involved in creating a custom termcap entry. Plus, you can optionally customize the termcap generated for the windows. You have to place these commands

in one of the screenrc startup files, as they are meaningless once the terminal emulator is booted.

If your system uses the terminfo database rather than termcap, **screen** will understand the **terminfo** command, which has the same effects as the **termcap** command. Two separate commands are provided, as there are subtle syntactic differences, e.g. when parameter interpolation (using '%') is required. Note that the termcap names of the capabilities should also be used with the **terminfo** command.

In many cases, where the arguments are valid in both terminfo and termcap syntax, you can use the command **termcapinfo**, which is just a shorthand for a pair of **termcap** and **terminfo** commands with identical arguments.

The first argument specifies which terminal(s) should be affected by this definition. You can specify multiple terminal names by separating them with '|'s. Use '*' to match all terminals and 'vt*' to match all terminals that begin with 'vt'.

Each *tweak* argument contains one or more termcap defines (separated by ':'s) to be inserted at the start of the appropriate termcap entry, enhancing it or overriding existing values. The first tweak modifies your terminal's termcap, and contains definitions that your terminal uses to perform certain functions. Specify a null string to leave this unchanged (e.g. ""). The second (optional) tweak modifies all the window termcaps, and should contain definitions that screen understands (see Chapter 11 [Virtual Terminal], page 45).

16.4 Termcap Examples

Some examples:

```
termcap xterm*  xn:hs@
```

Informs **screen** that all terminals that begin with 'xterm' have firm auto-margins that allow the last position on the screen to be updated (xn), but they don't really have a status line (no 'hs' – append '@' to turn entries off). Note that we assume 'xn' for all terminal names that start with 'vt', but only if you don't specify a termcap command for that terminal.

```
termcap vt*  xn
termcap vt102|vt220  Z0=\E[?3h:Z1=\E[?3l
```

Specifies the firm-margined 'xn' capability for all terminals that begin with 'vt', and the second line will also add the escape-sequences to switch into (Z0) and back out of (Z1) 132-character-per-line mode if this is a VT102 or VT220. (You must specify Z0 and Z1 in your termcap to use the width-changing commands.)

```
termcap vt100  ""  l0=PF1:l1=PF2:l2=PF3:l3=PF4
```

This leaves your vt100 termcap alone and adds the function key labels to each window's termcap entry.

```
termcap h19|z19  am@:im=\E@:ei=\EO  dc=\E[P
```

Takes a h19 or z19 termcap and turns off auto-margins (am@) and enables the insert mode (im) and end-insert (ei) capabilities (the '@' in the '**im**' string is after the '=', so it is part of the string). Having the '**im**' and '**ei**' definitions put into your terminal's termcap will cause screen to automatically advertise the character-insert capability in each window's termcap. Each window will also get the delete-character capability (dc) added to its termcap, which screen will translate into a line-update for the terminal (we're pretending it doesn't support character deletion).

If you would like to fully specify each window's termcap entry, you should instead set the $SCREENCAP variable prior to running screen. See Chapter 11 [Virtual Terminal], page 45, for the details of the screen terminal emulation. See Section "Termcap" in *The Termcap Manual*, for more information on termcap definitions.

16.5 Special Terminal Capabilities

The following table describes all terminal capabilities that are recognized by screen and are not in the termcap manual (see Section "Termcap" in *The Termcap Manual*). You can place these capabilities in your termcap entries (in '/etc/termcap') or use them with the commands termcap, terminfo and termcapinfo in your screenrc files. It is often not possible to place these capabilities in the terminfo database.

'LP'   (bool)
          Terminal has VT100 style margins ('magic margins'). Note that this capability is obsolete — screen now uses the standard 'xn' instead.

'Z0'   (str)
          Change width to 132 columns.

'Z1'   (str)
          Change width to 80 columns.

'WS'   (str)
          Resize display. This capability has the desired width and height as arguments. SunView(tm) example: '\E[8;%d;%dt'.

'NF'   (bool)
          Terminal doesn't need flow control. Send ^S and ^Q direct to the application. Same as flow off. The opposite of this capability is 'nx'.

'G0'   (bool)
          Terminal can deal with ISO 2022 font selection sequences.

'S0'   (str)
          Switch charset 'G0' to the specified charset. Default is '\E(%.'.

'E0'   (str)
          Switch charset 'G0' back to standard charset. Default is '\E(B'.

'C0'   (str)
          Use the string as a conversion table for font 0. See the 'ac' capability for more details.

'CS'   (str)
          Switch cursor-keys to application mode.

'CE'   (str)
          Switch cursor-keys to cursor mode.

'AN'   (bool)
          Enable autonuke for displays of this terminal type. (see Section 16.6 [Autonuke], page 73).

'OL'   (num)
                Set the output buffer limit. See the 'obuflimit' command (see Section 16.7
                [Obuflimit], page 73) for more details.

'KJ'   (str)
                Set the encoding of the terminal.   See the 'encoding' command (see
                Section 11.11 [Character Processing], page 52) for valid encodings.

'AF'   (str)
                Change character foreground color in an ANSI conform way. This capability
                will almost always be set to '\E[3%dm' ('\E[3%p1%dm' on terminfo machines).

'AB'   (str)
                Same as 'AF', but change background color.

'AX'   (bool)
                Does understand ANSI set default fg/bg color ('\E[39m / \E[49m').

'XC'   (str)
                Describe a translation of characters to strings depending on the current font.
                (see Section 16.8 [Character Translation], page 74).

'XT'   (bool)
                Terminal understands special xterm sequences (OSC, mouse tracking).

'C8'   (bool)
                Terminal needs bold to display high-intensity colors (e.g. Eterm).

'TF'   (bool)
                Add missing capabilities to the termcap/info entry. (Set by default).

16.6 Autonuke

autonuke *state*   [Command]
                (none)
                Sets whether a clear screen sequence should nuke all the output that has not been
                written to the terminal. See Section 16.7 [Obuflimit], page 73. This property is set
                per display, not per window.

defautonuke *state*   [Command]
                (none)
                Same as the **autonuke** command except that the default setting for new displays is
                also changed. Initial setting is **off**. Note that you can use the special **AN** terminal
                capability if you want to have a terminal type dependent setting.

16.7 Obuflimit

obuflimit [*limit*]   [Command]
                (none)
                If the output buffer contains more bytes than the specified limit, no more data will
                be read from the windows. The default value is 256. If you have a fast display (like
                xterm), you can set it to some higher value. If no argument is specified, the current
                setting is displayed. This property is set per display, not per window.

`defobuflimit` *limit*   [Command]
> (none)
>> Same as the `obuflimit` command except that the default setting for new displays
>> is also changed. Initial setting is 256 bytes. Note that you can use the special `OL`
>> terminal capability if you want to have a terminal type dependent limit.

16.8 Character Translation

`Screen` has a powerful mechanism to translate characters to arbitrary strings depending on
the current font and terminal type. Use this feature if you want to work with a common
standard character set (say ISO8851-latin1) even on terminals that scatter the more unusual
characters over several national language font pages.

Syntax:

> XC=<*charset-mapping*>{,,<*charset-mapping*>}
> <*charset-mapping*> := <*designator*><*template*>{,<*mapping*>}
> <*mapping*> := <*char-to-be-mapped*><*template-arg*>

The things in braces may be repeated any number of times.

A <*charset-mapping*> tells screen how to map characters in font <*designator*> ('B': Ascii,
'A': UK, 'K': german, etc.) to strings. Every <*mapping*> describes to what string a single
character will be translated. A template mechanism is used, as most of the time the codes
have a lot in common (for example strings to switch to and from another charset). Each
occurrence of '%' in <*template*> gets substituted with the *template-arg* specified together
with the character. If your strings are not similar at all, then use '%' as a template and
place the full string in <*template-arg*>. A quoting mechanism was added to make it possible
to use a real '%'. The '\' character quotes the special characters '\', '%', and ','.

Here is an example:

> `termcap hp700 'XC=B\E(K%\E(B,\304[,\326\\\,\334]'`

This tells `screen`, how to translate ISOlatin1 (charset 'B') upper case umlaut characters
on a `hp700` terminal that has a German charset. '\304' gets translated to '\E(K[\E(B' and
so on. Note that this line gets parsed *three* times before the internal lookup table is built,
therefore a lot of quoting is needed to create a single '\'.

Another extension was added to allow more emulation: If a mapping translates the un-
quoted '%' char, it will be sent to the terminal whenever screen switches to the corresponding
<*designator*>. In this special case the template is assumed to be just '%' because the charset
switch sequence and the character mappings normally haven't much in common.

This example shows one use of the extension:

> `termcap xterm 'XC=K%,%\E(B,[\304,\\\\\326,]\334'`

Here, a part of the German ('K') charset is emulated on an xterm. If screen has to change
to the 'K' charset, '\E(B' will be sent to the terminal, i.e. the ASCII charset is used instead.
The template is just '%', so the mapping is straightforward: '[' to '\304', '\' to '\326', and
']' to '\334'.

17 The Message Line

screen displays informational messages and other diagnostics in a *message line* at the bottom of the screen. If your terminal has a status line defined in its termcap, screen will use this for displaying its messages, otherwise the last line of the screen will be temporarily overwritten and output will be momentarily interrupted. The message line is automatically removed after a few seconds delay, but it can also be removed early (on terminals without a status line) by beginning to type.

17.1 Using the message line from your program

The message line facility can be used by an application running in the current window by means of the ANSI *Privacy message* control sequence. For instance, from within the shell, try something like:

```
echo "<ESC>^Hello world from window $WINDOW<ESC>\"
```

where '<ESC>' is ASCII ESC and the '^' that follows it is a literal caret or up-arrow.

17.2 Hardware Status Line

`hardstatus` [*state*]	[Command]
`hardstatus` [always]lastline|message|ignore [*string*]	[Command]
`hardstatus string` [*string*]	[Command]

> (none)
>
> This command configures the use and emulation of the terminal's hardstatus line. The first form toggles whether **screen** will use the hardware status line to display messages. If the flag is set to 'off', these messages are overlaid in reverse video mode at the display line. The default setting is 'on'.
>
> The second form tells screen what to do if the terminal doesn't have a hardstatus line (i.e. the termcap/terminfo capabilities "hs", "ts", "fs" and "ds" are not set). If the type **lastline** is used, screen will reserve the last line of the display for the hardstatus. **message** uses **screen**'s message mechanism and **ignore** tells **screen** never to display the hardstatus. If you prepend the word **always** to the type (e.g., **alwayslastline**), **screen** will use the type even if the terminal supports a hardstatus line.
>
> The third form specifies the contents of the hardstatus line. **%h** is used as default string, i.e., the stored hardstatus of the current window (settable via 'ESC]0;^G' or 'ESC_\\') is displayed. You can customize this to any string you like including string escapes (see Chapter 21 [String Escapes], page 89). If you leave out the argument *string*, the current string is displayed.
>
> You can mix the second and third form by providing the string as additional argument.

17.3 Display Last Message

`lastmsg`	[Command]

> (*C-a* m, *C-a C-m*)
>
> Repeat the last message displayed in the message line. Useful if you're typing when a message appears, because (unless your terminal has a hardware status line) the message goes away when you press a key.

17.4 Message Wait

`msgminwait` *sec*   [Command]
> (none)
>
> Defines the time **screen** delays a new message when another is currently displayed.
> Defaults to 1 second.

`msgwait` *sec*   [Command]
> (none)
>
> Defines the time a message is displayed, if **screen** is not disturbed by other activity.
> Defaults to 5 seconds.

18 Logging

This section describes the commands for keeping a record of your session.

18.1 hardcopy

hardcopy [-h] [*file*]   [Command]
    (*C-a h, C-a C-h*)
    Writes out the currently displayed image to the file *file*, or, if no filename is speci-
    fied, to 'hardcopy.*n*' in the default directory, where *n* is the number of the current
    window. This either appends or overwrites the file if it exists, as determined by the
    hardcopy_append command. If the option -h is specified, dump also the contents of
    the scrollback buffer.

hardcopy_append *state*   [Command]
    (none)
    If set to 'on', screen will append to the 'hardcopy.*n*' files created by the command
    hardcopy; otherwise, these files are overwritten each time.

hardcopydir *directory*   [Command]
    (none)
    Defines a directory where hardcopy files will be placed. If unset, hardcopys are
    dumped in screen's current working directory.

18.2 log

deflog *state*   [Command]
    (none)
    Same as the log command except that the default setting for new windows is changed.
    Initial setting is 'off'.

log [*state*]   [Command]
    (*C-a H*)
    Begins/ends logging of the current window to the file 'screenlog.*n*' in the window's
    default directory, where *n* is the number of the current window. This filename can be
    changed with the 'logfile' command. If no parameter is given, the logging state is
    toggled. The session log is appended to the previous contents of the file if it already
    exists. The current contents and the contents of the scrollback history are not included
    in the session log. Default is 'off'.

logfile *filename*   [Command]
logfile *flush secs*   [Command]
    (none)
    Defines the name the log files will get. The default is 'screenlog.%n'. The second
    form changes the number of seconds screen will wait before flushing the logfile buffer
    to the file-system. The default value is 10 seconds.

`logtstamp` [*state*]   [Command]
`logtstamp after` *secs*   [Command]
`logtstamp string` *string*   [Command]

    (none)

    This command controls logfile time-stamp mechanism of screen. If time-stamps are turned 'on', screen adds a string containing the current time to the logfile after two minutes of inactivity. When output continues and more than another two minutes have passed, a second time-stamp is added to document the restart of the output. You can change this timeout with the second form of the command. The third form is used for customizing the time-stamp string ('`-- %n:%t -- time-stamp -- %M/%d/%y %c:%s --\n`' by default).

19 Startup

This section describes commands which are only useful in the '.screenrc' file, for use at startup.

19.1 echo

echo ['-n'] *message*   [Command]
> (none)
>
> The echo command may be used to annoy **screen** users with a 'message of the day'. Typically installed in a global screenrc. The option '-n' may be used to suppress the line feed. See also **sleep**. Echo is also useful for online checking of environment variables.

19.2 sleep

sleep *num*   [Command]
> (none)
>
> This command will pause the execution of a .screenrc file for *num* seconds. Keyboard activity will end the sleep. It may be used to give users a chance to read the messages output by **echo**.

19.3 Startup Message

startup_message *state*   [Command]
> (none)
>
> Select whether you want to see the copyright notice during startup. Default is 'on', as you probably noticed.

20 Miscellaneous commands

The commands described here do not fit well under any of the other categories.

20.1 At

at [*identifier*][#| *| %] *command* [*args*]   [Command]

> (none)
>
> Execute a command at other displays or windows as if it had been entered there. **At** changes the context (the 'current window' or 'current display' setting) of the command. If the first parameter describes a non-unique context, the command will be executed multiple times. If the first parameter is of the form '*identifier**' then identifier is matched against user names. The command is executed once for each display of the selected user(s). If the first parameter is of the form '*identifier*%' identifier is matched against displays. Displays are named after the ttys they attach. The prefix '/dev/' or '/dev/tty' may be omitted from the identifier. If *identifier* has a # or nothing appended it is matched against window numbers and titles. Omitting an identifier in front of the #, * or % character selects all users, displays or windows because a prefix-match is performed. Note that on the affected display(s) a short message will describe what happened. Note that the # character works as a comment introducer when it is preceded by whitespace. This can be escaped by prefixing # with a \. Permission is checked for the initiator of the **at** command, not for the owners of the affected display(s). Caveat: When matching against windows, the command is executed at least once per window. Commands that change the internal arrangement of windows (like **other**) may be called again. In shared windows the command will be repeated for each attached display. Beware, when issuing toggle commands like **login**! Some commands (e.g. ***Qprocess**) require that a display is associated with the target windows. These commands may not work correctly under **at** looping over windows.

20.2 Break

break [*duration*]   [Command]

> (none)
>
> Send a break signal for *duration**0.25 seconds to this window. For non-Posix systems the time interval is rounded up to full seconds. Most useful if a character device is attached to the window rather than a shell process (see Section 6.6 [Window Types], page 26). The maximum duration of a break signal is limited to 15 seconds.

pow_break   [Command]

> (none)
>
> Reopen the window's terminal line and send a break condition.

breaktype [*tcsendbreak*| *TIOCSBRK*| *TCSBRK*]   [Command]

> (none)
>
> Choose one of the available methods of generating a break signal for terminal devices. This command should affect the current window only. But it still behaves identical

to `defbreaktype`. This will be changed in the future. Calling `breaktype` with no parameter displays the break setting for the current window.

defbreaktype [*tcsendbreak*| *TIOCSBRK*| *TCSBRK*]   [Command]
  (none)
  Choose one of the available methods of generating a break signal for terminal devices opened afterwards. The preferred methods are `tcsendbreak` and `TIOCSBRK`. The third, `TCSBRK`, blocks the complete `screen` session for the duration of the break, but it may be the only way to generate long breaks. `tcsendbreak` and `TIOCSBRK` may or may not produce long breaks with spikes (e.g. 4 per second). This is not only system dependent, this also differs between serial board drivers. Calling `defbreaktype` with no parameter displays the current setting.

20.3 Debug

debug [*on*| *off*]   [Command]
  (none)
  Turns runtime debugging on or off. If `screen` has been compiled with option `-DDEBUG` debugging is available and is turned on per default. Note that this command only affects debugging output from the main 'SCREEN' process correctly. Debug output from attacher processes can only be turned off once and forever.

20.4 License

license   [Command]
  (none)
  Display the disclaimer page. This is done whenever `screen` is started without options, which should be often enough.

20.5 Nethack

nethack *state*   [Command]
  (none)
  Changes the kind of error messages used by `screen`. When you are familiar with the game `nethack`, you may enjoy the nethack-style messages which will often blur the facts a little, but are much funnier to read. Anyway, standard messages often tend to be unclear as well.

  This option is only available if `screen` was compiled with the NETHACK flag defined (see Chapter 26 [Installation], page 101). The default setting is then determined by the presence of the environment variable `$NETHACKOPTIONS`.

20.6 Nonblock

nonblock [`state`| `numsecs`]   [Command]
  Tell screen how to deal with user interfaces (displays) that cease to accept output. This can happen if a user presses ^S or a TCP/modem connection gets cut but no hangup is received. If nonblock is `off` (this is the default) screen waits until

the display restarts to accept the output. If nonblock is **on**, screen waits until the timeout is reached (**on** is treated as 1s). If the display still doesn't receive characters, screen will consider it "blocked" and stop sending characters to it. If at some time it restarts to accept characters, screen will unblock the display and redisplay the updated window contents.

defnonblock *state* | *numsecs*   [Command]

Same as the **nonblock** command except that the default setting for displays is changed. Initial setting is **off**.

20.7 Number

number [*n*]   [Command]

(*C-a N*)

Change the current window's number. If the given number *n* is already used by another window, both windows exchange their numbers. If no argument is specified, the current window number (and title) is shown.

20.8 Silence

silence [*state* | *sec*]   [Command]

(none)

Toggles silence monitoring of windows. When silence is turned on and an affected window is switched into the background, you will receive the silence notification message in the status line after a specified period of inactivity (silence). The default timeout can be changed with the **silencewait** command or by specifying a number of seconds instead of **on** or **off**. Silence is initially off for all windows.

defsilence *state*   [Command]

(none)

Same as the **silence** command except that the default setting for new windows is changed. Initial setting is 'off'.

silencewait *seconds*   [Command]

(none)

Define the time that all windows monitored for silence should wait before displaying a message. Default is 30 seconds.

20.9 Time

time [*string*]   [Command]

(*C-a t, C-a C-t*)

Uses the message line to display the time of day, the host name, and the load averages over 1, 5, and 15 minutes (if this is available on your system). For window-specific information use **info** (see Section 11.6 [Info], page 50). If a *string* is specified, it changes the format of the time report like it is described in the string escapes chapter (see Chapter 21 [String Escapes], page 89). Screen uses a default of '%c:%s %M %d %H%? %l%?'.

20.10 Verbose

verbose [*on* | *off*]   [Command]
> If verbose is switched on, the command name is echoed, whenever a window is created (or resurrected from zombie state). Default is off. Without parameter, the current setting is shown.

20.11 Version

version   [Command]
> (C-a v)
> Display the version and modification date in the message line.

20.12 Zombie

zombie [*keys* [*onerror*]]   [Command]
defzombie [*keys*]   [Command]
> (none)
> Per default windows are removed from the window list as soon as the windows process (e.g. shell) exits. When a string of two keys is specified to the zombie command, 'dead' windows will remain in the list. The kill command may be used to remove the window. Pressing the first key in the dead window has the same effect. Pressing the second key, however, screen will attempt to resurrect the window. The process that was initially running in the window will be launched again. Calling zombie without parameters will clear the zombie setting, thus making windows disappear when the process terminates.
>
> As the zombie setting is affected globally for all windows, this command should only be called defzombie. Until we need this as a per window setting, the commands zombie and defzombie are synonymous.
>
> Optionally you can put the word onerror after the keys. This will cause screen to monitor exit status of the process running in the window. If it exits normally ('0'), the window disappears. Any other exit value causes the window to become a zombie.

20.13 Printcmd

printcmd [*cmd*]   [Command]
> (none)
> If *cmd* is not an empty string, screen will not use the terminal capabilities po/pf for printing if it detects an ansi print sequence ESC [5 i, but pipe the output into *cmd*. This should normally be a command like 'lpr' or 'cat > /tmp/scrprint'. Printcmd without an argument displays the current setting. The ansi sequence ESC \ ends printing and closes the pipe.
>
> Warning: Be careful with this command! If other user have write access to your terminal, they will be able to fire off print commands.

20.14 Sorendition

`sorendition [`*`attr [color]`*`]`   [Command]
> (none)
> Change the way screen does highlighting for text marking and printing messages. See
> the chapter about string escapes (see Chapter 21 [String Escapes], page 89) for the
> syntax of the modifiers. The default is currently '`=s dd`' (standout, default colors).

20.15 Attrcolor

`attrcolor` *`attrib`* `[`*`attribute/color-modifier`*`]`   [Command]
> (none)
> This command can be used to highlight attributes by changing the color of the text. If
> the attribute *attrib* is in use, the specified attribute/color modifier is also applied. If
> no modifier is given, the current one is deleted. See the chapter about string escapes
> (see Chapter 21 [String Escapes], page 89) for the syntax of the modifier. Screen
> understands two pseudo-attributes, `i` stands for high-intensity foreground color and
> `I` for high-intensity background color.
>
> Examples:
>
> `attrcolor b "R"`
> > Change the color to bright red if bold text is to be printed.
>
> `attrcolor u "-u b"`
> > Use blue text instead of underline.
>
> `attrcolor b ".I"`
> > Use bright colors for bold text. Most terminal emulators do this already.
>
> `attrcolor i "+b"`
> > Make bright colored text also bold.

20.16 Setsid

`setsid` *`state`*   [Command]
> (none)
> Normally screen uses different sessions and process groups for the windows. If setsid
> is turned `off`, this is not done anymore and all windows will be in the same process
> group as the screen backend process. This also breaks job-control, so be careful. The
> default is `on`, of course. This command is probably useful only in rare circumstances.

20.17 Eval

`eval` *`command1`* `[`*`command2`* ...]`   [Command]
> (none)
> Parses and executes each argument as separate command.

20.18 Maxwin

maxwin *n*   [Command]
>   (none)
>   Set the maximum window number screen will create. Doesn't affect already existing
>   windows. The number may only be decreased.

20.19 Backtick

backtick *id lifespan autorefresh command* [*args*]   [Command]
backtick *id*   [Command]
>   (none)
>   Program the backtick command with the numerical id *id*. The output of such a
>   command is used for substitution of the %' string escape (see Chapter 21 [String
>   Escapes], page 89). The specified *lifespan* is the number of seconds the output is
>   considered valid. After this time, the command is run again if a corresponding string
>   escape is encountered. The *autorefresh* parameter triggers an automatic refresh for
>   caption and hardstatus strings after the specified number of seconds. Only the last
>   line of output is used for substitution.
>
>   If both the *lifespan* and the *autorefresh* parameters are zero, the backtick program is
>   expected to stay in the background and generate output once in a while. In this case,
>   the command is executed right away and screen stores the last line of output. If a
>   new line gets printed screen will automatically refresh the hardstatus or the captions.
>
>   The second form of the command deletes the backtick command with the numerical
>   id *id*.

20.20 Screen Saver

idle [*timeout* [*cmd args*]]   [Command]
>   (none)
>   Sets a command that is run after the specified number of seconds inactivity is reached.
>   This command will normally be the blanker command to create a screen blanker, but
>   it can be any screen command. If no command is specified, only the timeout is set.
>   A timeout of zero (ot the special timeout off) disables the timer. If no arguments
>   are given, the current settings are displayed.

blanker   [Command]
>   (none)
>   Activate the screen blanker. First the screen is cleared. If no blanker program is
>   defined, the cursor is turned off, otherwise, the program is started and it's output is
>   written to the screen. The screen blanker is killed with the first keypress, the read
>   key is discarded.
>
>   This command is normally used together with the idle command.

blankerprg [*program args*]   [Command]
>   Defines a blanker program. Disables the blanker program if no arguments are given.

20.21 Zmodem

zmodem [*off* | *auto* | *catch* | *pass*]	[Command]
zmodem *sendcmd* [*string*]	[Command]
zmodem *recvcmd* [*string*]	[Command]

(none)

Define zmodem support for screen. Screen understands two different modes when it detects a zmodem request: `pass` and `catch`. If the mode is set to `pass`, screen will relay all data to the attacher until the end of the transmission is reached. In `catch` mode screen acts as a zmodem endpoint and starts the corresponding rz/sz commands. If the mode is set to `auto`, screen will use `catch` if the window is a tty (e.g. a serial line), otherwise it will use `pass`.

You can define the templates screen uses in `catch` mode via the second and the third form.

Note also that this is an experimental feature.

21 String Escapes

Screen provides an escape mechanism to insert information like the current time into messages or file names. The escape character is % with one exception: inside of a window's hardstatus ^% (^E) is used instead.

Here is the full list of supported escapes:

%	the escape character itself
a	either am or pm
A	either AM or PM
c	current time HH:MM in 24h format
C	current time HH:MM in 12h format
d	day number
D	weekday name
f	flags of the window
F	sets %? to true if the window has the focus
h	hardstatus of the window
H	hostname of the system
l	current load of the system
m	month number
M	month name
n	window number
s	seconds
S	session name
t	window title
u	all other users on this window
w	all window numbers and names. With − qualifier: up to the current window; with + qualifier: starting with the window after the current one.
W	all window numbers and names except the current one
y	last two digits of the year number
Y	full year number
?	the part to the next %? is displayed only if a % escape inside the part expands to a non-empty string
:	else part of %?

=   pad the string to the display's width (like TeX's hfill). If a number is specified, pad to the percentage of the window's width. A 0 qualifier tells screen to treat the number as absolute position. You can specify to pad relative to the last absolute pad position by adding a + qualifier or to pad relative to the right margin by using -. The padding truncates the string if the specified position lies before the current position. Add the L qualifier to change this.

<   same as %= but just do truncation, do not fill with spaces

>   mark the current text position for the next truncation. When screen needs to do truncation, it tries to do it in a way that the marked position gets moved to the specified percentage of the output area. (The area starts from the last absolute pad position and ends with the position specified by the truncation operator.) The L qualifier tells screen to mark the truncated parts with '...'.

{   attribute/color modifier string terminated by the next }

'   Substitute with the output of a 'backtick' command. The length qualifier is misused to identify one of the commands. See Section 20.19 [Backtick], page 86.

The c and C escape may be qualified with a 0 to make screen use zero instead of space as fill character. The n and = escapes understand a length qualifier (e.g. %3n), D and M can be prefixed with L to generate long names, w and W also show the window flags if L is given.

An attribute/color modifier is is used to change the attributes or the color settings. Its format is '[attribute modifier] [color description]'. The attribute modifier must be prefixed by a change type indicator if it can be confused with a color description. The following change types are known:

+   add the specified set to the current attributes

−   remove the set from the current attributes

!   invert the set in the current attributes

=   change the current attributes to the specified set

The attribute set can either be specified as a hexadecimal number or a combination of the following letters:

d   dim

u   underline

b   bold

r   reverse

s   standout

B   blinking

Colors are coded either as a hexadecimal number or two letters specifying the desired background and foreground color (in that order). The following colors are known:

k   black

r   red

g	green
y	yellow
b	blue
m	magenta
c	cyan
w	white
d	default color
.	leave color unchanged

The capitalized versions of the letter specify bright colors. You can also use the pseudo-color 'i' to set just the brightness and leave the color unchanged.

A one digit/letter color description is treated as foreground or background color dependent on the current attributes: if reverse mode is set, the background color is changed instead of the foreground color. If you don't like this, prefix the color with a '.'. If you want the same behavior for two-letter color descriptions, also prefix them with a '.'.

As a special case, '%{-}' restores the attributes and colors that were set before the last change was made (i.e. pops one level of the color-change stack).

Examples:

'G'	set color to bright green
'+b r'	use bold red
'= yd'	clear all attributes, write in default color on yellow background.

'%-Lw%{= BW}%50>%n%f* %t%{-}%+Lw%<'
:   The available windows centered at the current win dow and truncated to the available width. The current window is displayed white on blue. This can be used with 'hardstatus alwayslastline'.

'%?%F%{.R.}%?%3n %t%? [%h]%?'
:   The window number and title and the window's hardstatus, if one is set. Also use a red background if this is the active focus. Useful for 'caption string'.

22 Environment Variables

COLUMNS   Number of columns on the terminal (overrides termcap entry).

HOME   Directory in which to look for .screenrc.

LINES   Number of lines on the terminal (overrides termcap entry).

LOCKPRG   Screen lock program.

NETHACKOPTIONS
              Turns on **nethack** option.

PATH   Used for locating programs to run.

SCREENCAP
              For customizing a terminal's TERMCAP value.

SCREENDIR
              Alternate socket directory.

SCREENRC   Alternate user screenrc file.

SHELL   Default shell program for opening windows (default '/bin/sh').

STY   Alternate socket name. If **screen** is invoked, and the environment variable STY
              is set, then it creates only a window in the running **screen** session rather than
              starting a new session.

SYSSCREENRC
              Alternate system screenrc file.

TERM   Terminal name.

TERMCAP   Terminal description.

WINDOW   Window number of a window (at creation time).

23 Files Referenced

'.../screen-4.?.??/etc/screenrc'
'.../screen-4.?.??/etc/etcscreenrc'
> Examples in the **screen** distribution package for private and global initialization files.

'$SYSSCREENRC'
'/local/etc/screenrc'
> **screen** initialization commands

'$SCREENRC'
'$HOME/.iscreenrc'
'$HOME/.screenrc'
> Read in after /local/etc/screenrc

'$SCREENDIR/S-*login*'
'/local/screens/S-*login*'
> Socket directories (default)

'/usr/tmp/screens/S-*login*'
> Alternate socket directories.

'*socket directory*/.termcap'
> Written by the **dumptermcap** command

'/usr/tmp/screens/screen-exchange or'
'/tmp/screen-exchange'
> **screen** interprocess communication buffer

'hardcopy.[0-9]'
> Screen images created by the hardcopy command

'screenlog.[0-9]'
> Output log files created by the log command

'/usr/lib/terminfo/?/* or'
'/etc/termcap'
> Terminal capability databases

'/etc/utmp'
> Login records

'$LOCKPRG'
> Program for locking the terminal.

24 Credits

Authors

=======

Originally created by Oliver Laumann, this latest version was produced by Wayne Davison, Juergen Weigert and Michael Schroeder.

Contributors

============

```
        Ken Beal (kbeal@amber.ssd.csd.harris.com),
        Rudolf Koenig (rfkoenig@informatik.uni-erlangen.de),
        Toerless Eckert (eckert@informatik.uni-erlangen.de),
        Wayne Davison (davison@borland.com),
        Patrick Wolfe (pat@kai.com, kailand!pat),
        Bart Schaefer (schaefer@cse.ogi.edu),
        Nathan Glasser (nathan@brokaw.lcs.mit.edu),
        Larry W. Virden (lvirden@cas.org),
        Howard Chu (hyc@hanauma.jpl.nasa.gov),
        Tim MacKenzie (tym@dibbler.cs.monash.edu.au),
        Markku Jarvinen (mta@{cc,cs,ee}.tut.fi),
        Marc Boucher (marc@CAM.ORG),
        Doug Siebert (dsiebert@isca.uiowa.edu),
        Ken Stillson (stillson@tsfsrv.mitre.org),
        Ian Frechett (frechett@spot.Colorado.EDU),
        Brian Koehmstedt (bpk@gnu.ai.mit.edu),
        Don Smith (djs6015@ultb.isc.rit.edu),
        Frank van der Linden (vdlinden@fwi.uva.nl),
        Martin Schweikert (schweik@cpp.ob.open.de),
        David Vrona (dave@sashimi.lcu.com),
        E. Tye McQueen (tye%spillman.UUCP@uunet.uu.net),
        Matthew Green (mrg@eterna.com.au),
        Christopher Williams (cgw@pobox.com),
        Matt Mosley (mattm@access.digex.net),
        Gregory Neil Shapiro (gshapiro@wpi.WPI.EDU),
        Jason Merrill (jason@jarthur.Claremont.EDU),
        Johannes Zellner (johannes@zellner.org),
        Pablo Averbuj (pablo@averbuj.com).
```

Version

=======

This manual describes version 4.1.0 of the **screen** program. Its roots are a merge of a custom version 2.3PR7 by Wayne Davison and several enhancements to Oliver Laumann's version 2.0. Note that all versions numbered 2.x are copyright by Oliver Laumann.

See also See Section 25.3 [Availability], page 100.

25 Bugs

Just like any other significant piece of software, **screen** has a few bugs and missing features. Please send in a bug report if you have found a bug not mentioned here.

25.1 Known Bugs

- 'dm' (delete mode) and 'xs' are not handled correctly (they are ignored). 'xn' is treated as a magic-margin indicator.

- **screen** has no clue about double-high or double-wide characters. But this is the only area where **vttest** is allowed to fail.

- It is not possible to change the environment variable $TERMCAP when reattaching under a different terminal type.

- The support of terminfo based systems is very limited. Adding extra capabilities to $TERMCAP may not have any effects.

- **screen** does not make use of hardware tabs.

- **screen** must be installed setuid root on most systems in order to be able to correctly change the owner of the tty device file for each window. Special permission may also be required to write the file '/etc/utmp'.

- Entries in '/etc/utmp' are not removed when **screen** is killed with SIGKILL. This will cause some programs (like "w" or "rwho") to advertise that a user is logged on who really isn't.

- **screen** may give a strange warning when your tty has no utmp entry.

- When the modem line was hung up, **screen** may not automatically detach (or quit) unless the device driver sends a HANGUP signal. To detach such a **screen** session use the -D or -d command line option.

- If a password is set, the command line options -d and -D still detach a session without asking.

- Both **breaktype** and **defbreaktype** change the break generating method used by all terminal devices. The first should change a window specific setting, where the latter should change only the default for new windows.

- When attaching to a multiuser session, the user's '.screenrc' file is not sourced. Each users personal settings have to be included in the '.screenrc' file from which the session is booted, or have to be changed manually.

- A weird imagination is most useful to gain full advantage of all the features.

25.2 Reporting Bugs

If you find a bug in **Screen**, please send electronic mail to 'screen@uni-erlangen.de', and also to 'bug-gnu-utils@prep.ai.mit.edu'. Include the version number of **Screen** which you are using. Also include in your message the hardware and operating system, the compiler used to compile, a description of the bug behavior, and the conditions that triggered the bug. Please recompile **screen** with the '-DDEBUG' options enabled, reproduce the bug, and have a look at the debug output written to the directory '/tmp/debug'. If necessary quote suspect passages from the debug output and show the contents of your 'config.h' if it matters.

25.3 Availability

`Screen` is available under the `GNU` copyleft.

The latest official release of `screen` available via anonymous ftp from 'prep.ai.mit.edu', 'nic.funet.fi' or any other `GNU` distribution site. The home site of `screen` is 'ftp.uni-erlangen.de (131.188.3.71)', in the directory 'pub/utilities/screen'. The subdirectory 'private' contains the latest beta testing release. If you want to help, send a note to screen@uni-erlangen.de.

26 Installation

Since **screen** uses pseudo-ttys, the select system call, and UNIX-domain sockets/named pipes, it will not run under a system that does not include these features of 4.2 and 4.3 BSD UNIX.

26.1 Socket Directory

The socket directory defaults either to '`$HOME/.screen`' or simply to '`/tmp/screens`' or preferably to '`/usr/local/screens`' chosen at compile-time. If **screen** is installed setuid root, then the administrator should compile screen with an adequate (not NFS mounted) `SOCKDIR`. If **screen** is not running setuid-root, the user can specify any mode 700 directory in the environment variable `$SCREENDIR`.

26.2 Compiling Screen

To compile and install screen:

The **screen** package comes with a **GNU Autoconf** configuration script. Before you compile the package run

`sh ./configure`

This will create a '`config.h`' and '`Makefile`' for your machine. If **configure** fails for some reason, then look at the examples and comments found in the '`Makefile.in`' and '`config.h.in`' templates. Rename '`config.status`' to '`config.status.machine`' when you want to keep configuration data for multiple architectures. Running **sh** **./config.status.machine** recreates your configuration significantly faster than rerunning **configure**.

Read through the "User Configuration" section of '`config.h`', and verify that it suits your needs. A comment near the top of this section explains why it's best to install screen setuid to root. Check for the place for the global '`screenrc`'-file and for the socket directory.

Check the compiler used in '`Makefile`', the prefix path where to install **screen**. Then run

`make`

If **make** fails to produce one of the files '`term.h`', '`comm.h`' or '`tty.c`', then use *filename.x*`.dist` instead. For additional information about installation of **screen** refer to the file '`INSTALLATION`', coming with this package.

Concept Index

Command Index

This is a list of all the commands supported by **screen**.

I

idle 86
ignorecase 56
info 50
ins_reg 58

K

kill 41

L

lastmsg 75
license 82
lockscreen 32
log 77
logfile 77
login 41
logtstamp 78

M

mapdefault 65
mapnotnext 65
maptimeout 66
markkeys 55
maxwin 86
meta 64
monitor 42
msgminwait 76
msgwait 76
multiuser 32

N

nethack 82
next 29
nonblock 82
number 83

O

obuflimit 73
only 37
other 29

P

partial 51
password 31
paste 57
pastefont 58
pow_break 81
pow_detach 31
pow_detach_msg 31
prev 29
printcmd 84

process 58

Q

quit 35

R

readbuf 59
readreg 58
redisplay 52
register 59
remove 37
removebuf 59
reset 52
resize 37

S

screen 25
scrollback 55
select 29
sessionname 34
setenv 26
setsid 85
shell 26
shelltitle 26
silence 83
silencewait 83
sleep 79
slowpaste 58
sorendition 85
source 9
split 37
startup_message 79
stuff 58
su 34
suspend 35

T

term 26
termcap 70
termcapinfo 70
terminfo 70
time 83
title 39

U

umask 33
unsetenv 26
utf8 53

V

vbell 50
vbell_msg 50

Keystroke Index

This is a list of the default key bindings.

The leading escape character (see Section 14.3 [Command Character], page 64) has been omitted from the key sequences, since it is the same for all bindings.

Short Contents

Table of Contents

vii

www.ingramcontent.com/pod-product-compliance
Lightning Source LLC
LaVergne TN
LVHW060145070326
832902LV00018B/2956